D0290476

Forging the Productivity Partnership

William Sandy

McGraw-Hill Publishing Company

New York   St. Louis   San Francisco   Auckland   Bogotá
Caracas   Hamburg   Lisbon   London   Madrid   Mexico
Milan   Montreal   New Delhi   Oklahoma City
Paris   San Juan   São Paulo   Singapore
Sydney   Tokyo   Toronto

Randall Library UNC-W

*Appreciatively dedicated to all who are part of
the ongoing human quest for completion . . .
closing the gap between where we are and where
we could be.*

Library of Congress Cataloging-in-Publication Data

Sandy, William.
    Forging the productivity partnership / by William Sandy.
      p. cm.
    ISBN 0-07-054676-2 :
    1. Organizational change.   2. Organizational effectiveness.
    3. Labor productivity.   4. Customer relations.   I. Title.
    HD58.8.S26   1990
    658.4'06--dc20   89-48841
                                                           CIP

Copyright © 1990 by William Sandy. All rights reserved. Printed in the
United States of America. Except as permitted under the United States
Copyright Act of 1976, no part of this publication may be reproduced or
distributed in any form or by any means, or stored in a data base or
retrieval system, without the prior written permission of the publisher.

1 2 3 4 5 6 7 8 9 0 DOC/DOC 8 9 5 4 3 2 1 0 9

ISBN 0-07-054676-2

*The sponsoring editor for this book was Jim Bessent, the editing supervisor was
Barbara Toniolo, the designer was Naomi Auerbach, and the production
supervisor was Dianne Walber. It was set in Baskerville. It was composed by the
McGraw-Hill Publishing Company Professional & Reference Division
composition unit.*

Printed and bound by R. R. Donnelly and Sons, Company.

*For more information about other McGraw-Hill materials,
call 1-800-2-MCGRAW in the United States. In other
countries, call your nearest McGraw-Hill office.*

HD
58.8
.S26
1990

Contents

Foreword

Having studied, taught, participated in, and written a great deal about organizational transformation, I know that establishing partnerships is the key to getting results. Large-scale change will not come from a few but from many people working together to put propulsion behind intentions.

Sandy's experiences and ideas are a natural companion to *The Transformational Leader*. When you recognize the magnitude of improvement that has to take place and think about the potentials of emerging techniques to reach people in the workplace, it's clear that *Forging the Productivity Partnership* addresses the issues and opportunities of the nineties. Leaders and potential leaders anywhere in the organization will learn how to make better use of the behavior-shaping, energy-mobilizing tools of our times.

NOEL M. TICHY *Author of* The Transformational Leader *and*
Professor of Organizational Behavior
and Human Resource Management,
University of Michigan Business School

Preface

The Business Imperative to Change
Forging the Productivity Partnership is designed to make a difference in the way *you* do business.

It's about people, business's most underused, mishandled, undervalued resource.

It's about satisfying customers by strengthening the capabilities of those who meet customers directly and those throughout the organization who provide support for such efforts.

It's about profiting by using fresh concepts, putting human nature and self-interest to work, and applying new learning concepts and communications technology to save time, money, and frustration.

It's about winning against world-class competitors in the emerging global marketplace.

Business today faces big problems and big change. Managers at all levels develop sound plans but continually fall short of results in ways that will repeat themselves until those in charge—and those who want to be in charge—see the patterns and act on them. The weak link in the chain is people performance. No organization, no unit within an organization, can accomplish any more than its employees have the ability and the will to achieve.

Why This Book? Why Me? Why Now?
Our work at Sandy Inc. puts us at the frontier of organizational change:

We *design and teach performance change* in some of the nation's most sophisticated companies.

We *observe real-world performance situations* in major corporations and collaborate with tough-minded managers in devising solutions.

We *learn performance improvement* by keeping abreast of developments in behavioral science, technology, education, and communications.

We *operate our own public company* and cope with many of the same issues of change affecting clients.

We see what goes right and what goes wrong. Over time, on the basis of accumulated experience, we see patterns, so we have the opportunity to crystallize a unique, multidimensional view of what needs to happen to truly mobilize human energies.

We see more than our share of bold champions as well as quiet heroes, business people who have courage and vision of extraordinary power.

Unlocking the Transforming Resources of the '90s

Forging the Productivity Partnership is constructed to be a step-by-step overview of how to create the "people advantage" for your organization or your part of the organization. It shows how to develop and implement a human performance improvement strategy that works in today's workplace and that shows up in such practical results as improved profit, higher market share, and greater customer satisfaction.

It shows how to get people to work together better—managers and staffs, different functional disciplines as they hand off their work to one another, even traditional adversaries—because nobody today can afford energies leaking out at the intersects where people blend their skills.

This book and the partnering strategies it contains are for business leaders at every organizational level:

1. For chief executives; chief operating officers; directors of marketing, sales, production, or other functions; union leaders; government officials; franchise holders; suppliers and their associations—whoever can see the entire canvas and influence organizationwide change.
2. For leaders of any size unit within an organization who are tired of waiting for the entire company to get its act together and who want their operation not only to improve in significant ways but to be a model for other entities within the organization or the industry.
3. For individuals who want to get their own acts together as the first step toward doing bigger things, who recognize that there are better, less stressful ways to get results.

The unique perspective of this book is that it sweeps across a range of considerations that many managers tend to think about separately. It will help you deal with business strategy, human resource development, training, communications, information systems, motivation, and recognition together so that their full powers are applied seamlessly, in ways that reinforce rather than contradict.

Each chapter combines concepts, ideas, self-help advice, examples, analytical tools, checklists for change, and exercises to apply the lessons to your own situation. Far from disconnected tidbits of counsel, the elements fit together into a total strategy of major and sustainable improvement.

Part 1 starts with defining what matters most to your customers, your business's reason for being. It deals with getting a handle on the problems you face. Your grasp of them should be clear enough that you can share any challenge and any potential solution in all its dimensions. True partnerships depend upon everybody's assessing every task, large or small, in terms of its opportunities and consequences. This fully dimensioned assessment process involves steps that many business books miss and that many change-minded managers hurry past, thus creating repetitive frustration. Part 1 lays the foundation for enduring partnerships and sustained change among producers, suppliers, consumers, and distributors. It concentrates on giving managers a full understanding of what is accomplishable by the people they are counting on, whether those people are internal or external to the organization.

Part 2 is concerned with helping a business's leadership to deliver solutions that will help employees to win. The key is the individual, looking at every member of the organization as an audience of one, focusing on the interior commitments that individuals must make to reach their full potential. The emphasis is on giving feedback, interactive training, developing prescriptive answers that are tightly connected to your business objectives and the environment in which you compete. The capabilities and traps of emerging information technologies are revealed because they are key to getting more accomplished in less time. How to properly employ emotion and motivation in the process of business education and reeducation is thoroughly integrated.

Part 3 puts forward methods of recognizing results. Getting and giving value requires measuring what is happening, rewarding the application of new skills, and tracking profit return. The emphasis in Part 3 is on learning and communication as dynamic processes, continually raising sights, and continually reaping marketplace advantage through the way your people approach their work.

The three parts, then, rivet attention on the three crucial elements of serious improvement:

—Developing a clear understanding of the context in which you compete.
—Developing solutions that match the problems you define.
—Measuring and recognizing what happens.

Forging the Productivity Partnership can be a valuable guidebook for the 1990s and the century ahead, when the transforming resources in business enterprise will increasingly be people, information, new learning, and technology. How to manage the interplay of these resources, how to initiate the necessary partnerships, how to get people to do more of what matters—these are the themes of our exploration. I hope this book does justice to the exhilaration and natural drama of the change process.

Acknowledgments

It's appropriate that a book about partnering should have many partners in its creation.

I would like to express my appreciation first of all to our clients, the restless leaders who over the years have given me access to their hopes, dreams, fears, problems, insights, and ideas, providing the real-world experiences in massive change upon which this book is based.

Working with several hundred professional colleagues at Sandy Corporation, I have had the unique opportunity to draw upon a wide range of skills and perspectives. Ray Ketchledge, Lynn Guerin, Andy McGill, Bob Bennett, Fred Strickland, and Peter Steffes are some of the many professionals who have helped shape core concepts, not just because they understand them, but because they devote their lives to these ideas.

Bill Giles, director of the School of Journalism at Louisiana State University and formerly director of publications at Sandy Corporation, executive editor and vice president of *The Detroit News*, and director of Management Programs of Dow Jones & Co., helped launch the developmental process on the right basis with his disciplined, probing questions and penchant to clarify meanings. Vicki Keeler, Judith Wilson, and Richard Giles have provided important research assistance. Dick Cavagnol, Bob Oren, and Sharon Haman developed many of the visuals.

I am indebted, also, to professional colleagues at the Instructional Systems Association (ISA), the American Society for Training and Development (ASTD), a number of Big 6 consulting firms with whom we have collaborated, and to my associates on the national alumni council of Harvard Business School. The leading-edge research of these organizations and of individuals too numerous to name has served as a continuing stimulus and inspiration.

I am particularly grateful to have a wife and a next generation of Sandys, and still another generation coming along behind them, who have turned out to be the kind of people I admire and like as well as love. To Alan, Lewis, Barbara, Carol, Kathy, Matthew, Charlotte, and Natalie—thanks for living the idea that "to be who you are and to become what you are capable of becoming is a major goal of life." Especial thanks go to my wife, Marjorie, who as a wife, mother, friend, and librarian, in every arena of human contact, is a giver, not a taker, the embodiment of a marvelous partner.

In addition, I am proud to have had the chance to begin my career with—and would like to credit—the man who was among the first to grasp the film industry's educational potential and who many consider to be the founding father of audiovisual business education, Jamison Handy.

Through family, clients, colleagues, friends and mentors, then, I have had the kinds of associations that make human development a continually wondrous and life-enhancing experience.

William Sandy

Introduction

*A man's reach should exceed his grasp ... or
what's a heaven for?*   ROBERT BROWNING

Change Incorporated

Let's look squarely at change. Big, revolutionary, all-encompassing
change. Change so vast and so deep that no part of your organization
will ever be quite the same again. This is the kind of upheaval business
must confront today.

Every day, managers face intense pressure to cope with the acceler-
ating pace of change, and they are growing increasingly concerned that
the skills and attitudes they bring to the workplace don't meet the demands.

Your Grip on Reality:
Crafting a Fully Dimensioned
Situational Assessment

In *The Guns of August* historian Barbara Tuchman tells the story of
why more casualties were suffered by both sides in the first month of
World War I than in the rest of the war.[1] The Germans had superior
forces and weaponry at that time. The French military command had a
tradition of "élan," meaning any retreat was considered a weakness of
will rather than sound military strategy. French generals, finding their
peers replaced at any suggestion of the magnitude of effort that might
be needed, stopped dealing with the real issues and moved their unpre-
pared armies forward into heavy casualties.

I told that story to a senior executive of a major corporation that was
emphasizing "positive attitude" without giving sufficient weight to root

1

causes and strategic issues. His discouraging response to this cautionary tale: "That's an interesting story. 'Elan' would make a wonderful name for one of our future products."

Big organizations are sometimes tempted to dispense with reality and try to bull their way to success. As one manager I know puts it, "All my life I've put square pegs into round holes. It's lucky I'm strong."

Current reality is *important* as a basis for any business initiative, but it is *imperative* when you are trying to mobilize people to improvements on a large scale. When mobilizing for significant performance improvement, you secure the right answers by starting with the right questions. Communications and training activities are means to an end, not ends in themselves. Before you start developing and implementing strategies of performance improvement, it is important to conduct a tough, practical analysis of the current business situation, what systems people call the "now state." Too many corporations are event-driven or calendar-driven instead of starting on the basis of what the organization truly needs at a particular point in time. There are periods when the organization needs time to absorb and integrate earlier initiatives, when the best action may be inaction.

The reason for a thorough, honest assessment of your situation is fundamental. Those who are being asked to change their ways of doing things and adopt a new approach are closer to their jobs—and therefore to the real challenges—than those at the policy levels of organizations. If the issues raised and the improvements targeted do not pass an instant, visceral test of practicality and credibility, then the minds and hearts of the people you are counting on will not be engaged.

Leaders of business organizations are usually talking to people who are on the payroll or who are otherwise dependent, so those people have to listen, but they don't have to believe. And in an era of downsizing and other economic turbulence, it is important that you respect the problems and the cynicism of anyone you are targeting for improved performance.

Make That Actionable Information

Situational information seems deceptively easy to pull together because most corporations are drowning in data. The real need, though, is for actionable information. This kind of information is not always easy to create. Frequently, layers of information obscure rather than clarify the real situations. It is a common complaint in large organizations: "We can't find what we know."

Your situational assessment should be candid, participative, and focused on practical yields:

1. So that you understand the challenges fully.

2. So you can address misconceptions. Until you do, when you are working with people, their perception *is* reality.

3. So you can begin the process of creating receptivity for change. This is a discovery process. Don't hurry past it. Face the challenges, raw and unvarnished, and you will find people far more willing to move on to new ways. Danger is a stimulus. Sharing problems candidly is a compliment to adults.

4. So that you get more people thinking creatively about solutions, especially the people who are closest to your customers and closest to the tasks at hand.

5. So you can accurately and vividly describe the situation to the people you expect to change it. For many people, the status quo is comfortable. The familiar is home to them. Getting people to move beyond where they are and what they have done calls for a clear and compelling description of the consequences of settling in, and of the urgency and gains of moving on.

6. So that you can use the language of the street, the language of the workplace, to describe solutions and lines of attack, building credibility and increasing your chances of igniting emotional commitment. Ride the trucks with the route people. Break bread with the people in the plant.

These are the concentrations of *Forging the Productivity Partnership*. We will continually move to the micro world of individual commitment and individualized prescriptions for growth. But for now, at the situational assessment stage, it is important to take a macro view of the forces shaping what your customers want and your employees need. Foremost among the forces to be inventoried are:

- How the world around you is changing
- How the work force is changing

You may have other questions. The main point is to look at the full dimensions of what you face—external reality, competitive reality, and what future reality is likely to be. Put yourself and key others in a position to see it all, simultaneously, like a winning quarterback sees the whole playing field or an experienced general sees the ebbs and flows of battle in order to sense where to mount the next attack.

If there is no precision in establishing baseline reality and carefully targeted improvements, the result is often unjustified optimism. The story is told of a medieval court jester who was sentenced to death by the king and earned a reprieve by promising to make the king's horse fly within six months. Found whistling the next day, the jester was asked why he wasn't worried. "Three things might happen," he said. "The king might die. The horse might die. Or I might really teach the horse to fly."

Changes in the Marketplace

The global nature of competition today means the rate of change can be expected to gather momentum, not abate. Your thinking about markets, problems, people, and competition needs to pick up both the tempo and turbulence of the times.

The market is changing, fast becoming a global marketplace. Companies find their customers continually demanding more quality and variety as they shop a worldwide array of goods pouring into the most affluent bazaar in the world.

The Japanese are showing the entire Pacific basin what can be accomplished with planning plus commitment. The European Community is preparing to blur national boundaries to achieve economies of scale. Even giant nations like China and the U.S.S.R. are making the transition to economic rather than military competition with capitalist nations.

Manufacturing is changing, with old plants being shut down, others opened, and still others being redesigned, sometimes filled with mind-boggling technology. Unfortunately, this too often happens without parallel investment in the human beings who must partner with such technologies. Technology is radically changing production, communications, and finance.

People are changing. Japanese, Russians, Yugoslavs, Taiwanese, Brazilians, Koreans, and others are aspiring to new living standards. Worldwide television and radio contact, computer linkages, audiocassettes, and other widely accessible methods of communication now dramatize the kind of affluence that becomes a model for industrializing nations. Americans too are changing as companies, industries, unions, government, and individuals respond to the new realities of global competitiveness.

Changes in the Work Force

The work force is changing with startling speed. This is true for blue collar and white collar, true for managers and union members alike.

In 1985, almost half of the work force was comprised of the stereotypical American breadwinner—U.S.-born, white, and male. Between 1985 and the dawn of the next century, new U.S.-born, white male entrants into the workplace will shrink to about 15 percent, fewer than one in six. There will be almost three times as many U.S.-born, white females starting work as white males. At the same time, about 27 million people, 15 percent of the work force, can be considered functionally illiterate, and that number will increase at the rate of 2.5 million people a year.

The aging of the work force carries profound economic implications. In 1952, when a worker chose to retire, there were 17 other workers assuming the productivity and tax payment responsibilities. At the turn of this century, for each retiree, there will be just one and a half workers.

As managers demand more of people in order to mobilize greater effort, there will be fewer of the select choices. To illustrate, for a job as seemingly straightforward as bank teller, Chemical Bank of New York recently found that its interview-to-hire ratio had increased to 40:1.

To attract the highest caliber people, the classic strategy is to create an excellent position. Excellent jobs attract excellent people. Right? But the structure of jobs is changing, again at an accelerated rate. About 10 percent of all jobs change in major ways each year. According to contemporary career planning, young people should expect six employers and three complete career changes during their working lifetimes. John Young, president of Hewlett-Packard, figures that today's workers can anticipate having to be completely retrained five times during their working years.[2]

Changes in Values

Attitudes and values are changing. Loyalty to individual employers has dropped sharply in the past decade. Younger members of the work force raised in affluent times have expectations of entitlements that raise the cost of labor significantly, so that perks constitute an ever-increasing percentage of total labor costs. Whatever the party in national office, the deficit and resistance to taxation accelerate the trend of asking business to absorb more and more health and other social costs. Given the complexity of the issues, the transition from the values of the "me generation" to the more collaborative style of a new "we generation" becomes an urgent priority.

Most important, our minds are changing, stretching to comprehend and cope with the implications of a world economy undergoing truly revolutionary change.

The changes we are up against are colossal and beyond our experience. What we're seeing—big trade deficits, huge capital accumulation abroad, dislocated industries, technological breakthroughs, trade legislation—represents the dawning of a new world economic order in which chaos becomes an everyday part of the business scene.

Mainstreaming the Human Resources Function

It is time for a change in how we manage and grow people. Operating managers need to take a strong hand so that business learning and organizational communication are tied tightly to business strategy.

More than ever, the highest payout task of management is to forge partnerships to accomplish results. Yet the literature is behind the times, treating people development as a narrow specialty rather than as part of mainstream business strategy.

Is it worth putting this much emphasis on people? Chances are you are not a professional educator and were delighted the day you put school behind you. You are not the chaplain. You are a business executive focused on results, under pressure to make things a lot better rapidly. You are searching for ways that create fresh marketplace advantage.

Is it really *practical* to make human performance central to business strategy? Ask Roger Smith. Chairman of General Motors during the eighties, Smith came up through the finance route, a career path that puts a premium on hard-core pragmatism. As he guided his organization through wrenching change, Smith came to a growing awareness of the importance of people. As he told *Fortune* magazine:

> If I had the opportunity to do everything over again, I would make exactly the same decision that I made in 1981 when I became chief executive. I'd begin to rebuild General Motors, inside out and from the bottom up, to turn it into a 21st-century corporation, one that would continue to be a global leader. But I sure wish I had done a better job of communicating with GM people. I'd do that differently a second time around and make sure they understood and shared my vision for the company. Then they would have known why I was tearing the place up, taking out whole divisions, changing our whole production structure. If people understand the *why*, they'll work at it. Like I say, I never got all this across. There we were, charging up the hill right on schedule, and I looked behind me and saw that many people were still at the bottom, trying to decide whether to come along.

Once he came to appreciate the central role of people in the change endeavor, Smith took decisive action to better the situation:

When I saw that our people didn't understand my vision for GM, I knew I had to go back and get them on board. And I did. We started a series of offsite meetings, away from the office and plants. We'd all sit down in groups of ten and talk things through. They'd ask questions, and they asked good ones too. Today everyone wants in on the vision. Believe me, this makes me feel better than any time in my 40 years at GM.[3]

Combating the Benign
Neglect of Human Resources

Part of the reason that this kind of enlightenment has been slow in coming to many organizations, and slower still to spread, is structural. Too many senior managers in American business have treated the development of their human resources with aloofness. For them, personnel matters have not been where the action is. Employee training, education, and communication of corporate goals have often been fragmented and impulsive. A manual here, a booklet there, a meeting, or an occasional seminar are typical of the piecemeal approach American corporations have taken to sharpening the most powerful weapon in their competitive arsenal.

But this is changing. Pioneering operational managers are beginning to see the mobilization of people toward strategic objectives as the mainstream success factor, their single best hope to win. Managers short of time find that if they don't have enough resources to face every problem in neat, sequential order, something amazing happens when you put people performance at or near the top of the agenda. A number of other problems go away because they are symptoms of not having people mobilized for results.

Harnessing Business
Knowledge

Some of the confusion, some of the scariness of today's challenges, comes from lack of comfort with the important new resources to confront change. Daniel Bell, professor of Sociology at Harvard University, points out that codification of theoretical knowledge is replacing capital and energy as the primary transforming resource. A *Fortune* report on future business growth points up the importance of "getting this new information into peoples' heads." Paul Strassman, former vice president of Xerox, is quoted in that same report as saying that by the turn of the century, 25 percent of the gross national product of the United States will be spent on education and professional training, compared with 10 percent today.[4] When learning, information, and the technology to deliver that learning become so central a resource, it is an important time for shirtsleeve operating managers, not just behavioral or communications specialists, to grasp the implications and to seize the levers of change.

Knowledge in the current "information age" is becoming understood in corporate strategies to be a driving business force. Learning and training now can be delivered to people at their workstations via computers or audio and video cassettes. Information can be packaged in specific, job-related ways, available when it's needed and delivered the way adults prefer to learn. What's more, instructional quality has improved significantly through user-friendly, interactive programming. New ways have been developed to evaluate reliably the effectiveness of instruction.

What this means is that human performance can be measurably improved to enhance overall organizational performance. But up to now, only a few companies have worked to make human performance an integral part of their business strategies. How to "hinge" those human and business strategies together is going to be the work of managers for years to come.

Checklist for Change

☑ Strategize performance improvement as one of your major ways to improve your business.

☑ Create a fully dimensioned situational assessment.

☑ Factor in the impact of global competition and turbulence.

☑ Understand how the work force is changing in terms of numbers, demographic composition, knowledge, and values.

Apply the Learning

Draw an organization chart that represents the skills and reporting relationships needed to meet emerging competitive conditions. Compare and contrast to your current organization chart.

PART 1

Forge a Customer-Driven Performance Strategy

The most important stage of large-scale performance change is the beginning, when situations are assessed and attitudes formed, when directions are determined and leaders are put into place, and when initiatives are formulated and described. These foundation steps should be carried forth in an atmosphere of mutual trust and respect, with findings and objectives explained in ways human beings can understand and act upon.

1

Do More
of What Matters
to Your Customers

Don't look back in anger or ahead in fear,
but around you with awareness.
                              JAMES THURBER

Toward a New Mind-Set

You are faced with the need for change. Where do you begin? How do you finally leave behind the debilitating procrastination? How do you end the eternal circling around problems, discussing them, debating them, but never really altering your world? How do you break the cycle of frustration that keeps repeating itself as new initiatives are begun with great fanfare and then slowly die, never to be heard from again. The business landscape is littered with rallying slogans and themes which live on as empty labels, without resources, leadership, or commitment, testimony to just one more intention gone awry. How do you jolt your organization out of this premature plateauing of effort, the comfort levels that human beings reach when danger signs are not clearly present or are just plain denied? How do you convince the entire organization that total change would be easier and more likely to succeed than fragmented efforts, that moving together into new methods with new energies is the best answer?

You focus right from the start on the two major drivers of your business success:

- How your business earns its profit
- What your customers put value on

Teach "Profit Ability"

Before the issues start to appear as intimidatingly complex, before the calendar becomes too full of activities, before managers begin loading employees down with specialized training, it is important to concentrate on the simple fact that employees are there to contribute to customer satisfaction and the profit that comes when customers buy and buy again.

Any organizational performance improvement strategy you may devise will ultimately show up in dozens or hundreds of different activities. But for the business force to truly be a force, the core skill to be learned is "profit ability," literally the ability of people to contribute to profit:

- To do more and better what matters to customers
- To do less of or differently what is unimportant or negative in the buying and ownership experience
- To consistently excel where it makes the biggest difference

This can be done if there is a sound basis of analysis.

All the other efforts of an organization—plans, meetings, processes, procedures, paperwork—are irrelevant if they don't gear into satisfying customer needs and wants. That's where the money comes from. That's where the profit is. That's reality.

The Path to Prosperity— A Road Less Traveled

Understanding the customer is more than analyzing or quantifying data. It is understanding why customers buy, how they come to market, how they are changing, and how the buying and ownership experiences are meeting their expectations.

Customer-driven reality includes understanding your competitors' customers and why they prefer to buy elsewhere. And it's comprehending the total market—those who ought to be your customers but never enter your orbit.

In any business that supplies services, the perception of customers *is* reality. You win or lose in the eyes of the customer and the customer's intention to repurchase or recommend.

There are three major ways for a business to improve its position:

1. Of course, most important is to *offer superior products or services.* Improvements designed in during R&D lay the groundwork for a lot of good things to start happening. Managers are keenly aware of the amount of time and attention lavished on this phase of business. At that, even when breakthroughs are achieved, very few product or service advantages last long without emulation in this age of quick copying.

2. *Reach out to your targeted market;* maximize the number of people to come in and consider your offerings. Advertising, merchandising, promotional supports and such incentives as coupons, rebates, premiums, special offers, inventory selection, and point-of-sale decor are all used extensively by you and your competitors. The danger here is that messages can become increasingly fragmented, expensive, and mutually neutralizing. For national organizations in the United States, for example, that involves the cost of trying to talk to as many as 250 million people in messages as short as 15 seconds, which are surrounded by the enormous clutter of everyone else's claims.

3. *Mobilize your business force for optimum marketplace advantage.* Of the three areas for significant improvement, this one is the frontier, the least-charted area, and one that is growing in strategic importance. Moreover, strides taken in business force creation and maintenance provide the underpinnings for progress in the other two areas.

You achieve impact and differentiation when performances in every phase of the business process are so consistently superior that they become reason for customer interest and loyalty. In a world in which it is increasingly difficult and expensive to earn share of mind, your people can achieve undivided attention and can create extraordinary impact just when it counts most, in your customers' everyday interactions with your organization.

Doing More of and Better What Really Matters

Nobody is going to be wonderful at everything. Imperfections and shortfalls characterize the human condition. As a manager, the goal is to concentrate on what matters most. How do you draw up this kind of assessment?

Go Straight to the Source—Your Customers

The best way to get a handle on the relevance of a performance improvement strategy to the issues you face is to ask your customers. This shouldn't be casual feedback. Diagnose customer satisfaction and track increases and declines with simple, clear, permanent indicators. Develop indexes that not only help you analyze statistical progress but also let you trace the people actions that contribute to buyer satisfaction or dissatisfaction.

The most important influences on customer satisfaction are the buying experience and the ownership experience. Customer satisfaction can be defined in a very simple and practical way: It's the willingness to buy again and to recommend to others.

Diagram the way that your customers come to market and reach their purchase decisions. Lay it out as a path, like a flowchart. How are they first influenced when they are in the purchase consideration phase? Who influences them and how as they get closer to the decision? What are the roles of various employees during their ownership experience? How does this influence intention to repurchase and/or to recommend your product or service?

Consider how these industrywide findings apply to your operation:[5]

- Thirty-three percent of households experience problems with purchases.
- Twenty-five percent of purchase decisions involve some problem.

Conclusion: Dissatisfaction is widespread.

- Between 70 and 90 percent of those experiencing a problem do not complain.
- Fewer than 5 percent of complaints about large-ticket durable goods or services ever reach the manufacturer.

Conclusion: Dissatisfaction is deeper than you may believe; much remains hidden.

- When complaints are satisfactorily resolved, repurchase intention averages 70 percent. When complaints are not resolved, intention drops to 46 percent. When a dissatisfied person doesn't complain, repurchase intention is lowest of all at 37 percent. Dissatisfied complainants tell twice as many people about their negative experiences as satisfied complainants tell about their positive interactions. A customer who has had a bad experience figures to tell 10 others. Listeners put twice as much weight on negative information as on positive information.

Conclusion: How customers feel is crucial to marketplace success.

- In service industries, for example, the four leading causes of customer dissatisfaction are:

  Lack of responsiveness in problem resolution (39 percent)

  Delays or interruptions in service delivery (36 percent)

  Unfriendly employees (33 percent)

  Errors in billing or delivery (32 percent)

Conclusion: The key is the work force. Problems will occur in any business, but positive attitude, fast response, and good information can keep most customers satisfied.

Broaden Your Concept of the Customer

In strategizing customer satisfaction, or "customer obsession," you need to broaden your definitions:

- Customers, plural, are different from each other by region, age, marital status, and values. What satisfies customers is tied to the level of expectation created by your product or service. People expect more from a premium-priced product or service; less from a clearly identified "cash and carry" transaction.

- Customers are more than the buyers of your finished products or services. On the way to creating that product or service, there is a chain of organizational interactions. Every person and function that is part of the chain needs to look at whoever receives their output as their customer. So when engineering hands off to manufacturing, there should be customer-satisfying actions every step of the way.

- While it is wise to track and avoid customer dissatisfaction, you should aspire to do more than make problems go away. The thrust should be to achieve customer impressions that are so consistently positive that they become visible reasons to buy, buy again, and recommend enthusiastically. This is the high payout task; your assessment should track when, where, and why you are being credited with the people edge.

Evaluating your performance versus customer needs is only the beginning of the assessment process. Truly understanding the situation has a number of other dimensions discussed in the next chapter. But this is the right place to begin. It is the most important indicator. And it is your best way to begin the process of turning adversaries into partners. Remember, management or staff, white collar or blue, specialist or field representative, headquarters or supplier—the customer is the one who is paying for everything and everyone. When you get people thinking about what matters to your customers, you also get them thinking about how your organization earns its profit.

No company is ever likely to be "the best" in everything. Focused strategy, however, calls for being the best in some thing or things that customers consider really important.

Tracking the Competition

Most organizations track their competitors in terms of market share or other numerical indicators. But what do you know about how the people in competitive organizations do their jobs? Nordstrom, Neiman-Marcus, Bloomingdale's, Sheraton, and Ritz Carlton are certainly examples of organizations that make superior people performance part of their fundamental strategy.

Your assessment of reality should also include some kind of organizational competitiveness process, a detailed systemic analysis of what your competitors are up to, where they are better, and how they are changing. Take every task that is part of your business and search out best practice in the industry. Define current superiority in the little things as well as the big ones.

Make the organizational competitiveness process an ongoing one, a perpetual scanning of who is good, better, and best on every important human criterion and every significant product or service characteristic.

Bob Stempel, the president of General Motors, urges product developers to think in terms of "millimeters of difference." Frequently such differences are designed in. But their importance in the marketplace depends upon the ease and power with which the selling organization can surface those differences with the customer during the buying decision process.

Don't restrict your search to head-to-head competition. Frequently this organizational competitiveness process should be done on a cross-industry basis, researching adjacent industries. For example, customer satisfaction practices in the hotel industry, where the user experience *is* the product, have direct transferability to such other industries as high-ticket durable goods.

Inventory best practices wherever they might be found. This kind of investigation should continually record, visually, via snapshots, video, or whatever, as well as by the more traditional words and numbers, examples of those superior business practices. This is more than an abstract research report. When you are ready to disseminate those superior ways of doing business, people who have become accustomed to older methods are going to need evidence of results and role models to follow.

Leave Your N-I-H at H-O-M-E

Taking off the blinders, jettisoning NIH, the "not invented here" attitude that "our way is best," is a very useful mind-set for serious change. Corporations can no longer afford to waste the by-products of fact-based program development. It is a waste to analyze your products versus your competitors' only to tell your sales force and your customers how and why you are better.

If your product comparison research is objective, systemic, and ongoing, you have another important yield: showing your product developers where you are falling short.

Develop a
Customer-Satisfaction Index

When through continual customer analysis and competitive scanning you get a real bead on where you stand in the eyes of the marketplace, you are ready to develop an index. This is a simple diagnostic graph that shows where you are in relation to customer expectations, competitors, and improvement goals. When the work force becomes accustomed to the format, they can move the indicators upward.

This isn't simply research. It is research designed to trigger long-term and large-scale performance improvement. So it is important that the indexes be designed to be diagnostic—to lead those who are paying attention to the indexes to a better understanding of the position-by-position contributions to superior scores. In that way, you can "teach the test," use the measurement process as a practical tool for those working to achieve superior results.

Consider the Speed of Change

The speed of innovation in your industry is a very important factor. It is possible that you and your people are improving at 30 miles per hour, when all around you, competitors are traveling at 60 miles per hour.

Conclusion:
A Process, Not a Program

In this fast-moving world, reality shifts abruptly, which is why organizational improvement is a process, not a program. Yesterday's advantages in how people do business become tomorrow's norms, and the day after that, somebody is doing it better. So you need to continually reassess reality, continually redefine and elevate standards of performance. That takes ongoing systemic process, not permanent notebooks frozen at one point in time. Computerized information and electronic publishing capabilities have important potentials to keep reality continually current and performance standards continually raised.

Facing reality is a shared responsibility. It's more than research; it's the beginning of the self-analysis and the forming of interior commitments that will be important to long-term, large-scale change. When the people on the receiving end of your training and communication efforts participate in the process of drawing accurate, realistic, current assessments, they are engaging in a discovery process. The importance of change and major improvement starts to form in the gut, the heart, and the mind.

Checklist for Change

- ☑ Start your assessment process with what matters most to your customers.

- ☑ Teach "profit ability," the ability that contributes directly to profit and customer satisfaction.

- ☑ Diagram how your customers come to the decision process—who and what influences them.

- ☑ Analyze your rate of dissatisfaction, remembering that complaints are only the tip of the iceberg. Most dissatisfied customers do not bother to complain.

- ☑ Analyze best competitive practice, especially how people do their jobs to satisfy customers.

☑ Analyze the specific, superior behaviors that, consistently practiced, could become part of your marketplace differentiation.

☑ Define the precise satisfiers that can create marketplace advantage.

☑ Apply the customer satisfaction analysis process to the handoffs from one function to another inside your organization.

☑ Gauge the rate of innovation and change around you, to make sure you are going at least at comparable speed.

Apply the Learning

Select one function in your company. Divide a sheet of paper into two columns. In column A, put down what you believe is important about that function. In column B, using the best available information, including a personal survey, put down what your customers believe is important. Compare for alignments and misalignments.

2
Understand the Challenges and Share Them

Organizations don't do things. People do.
D. QUINN MILLS

If you have a good grasp of what your customers want, why not just go do it? And if the people you're counting on aren't doing it the way you want, why not simply tell them?

If telling were the same as teaching, the world would be a very smart place. And if the view of headquarters or senior executives as summarized neatly in business plans were the total picture, the improvements would have happened a long time ago.

The single biggest reason that "answers" to challenges fall short, is that the right questions haven't been asked of the right people at the right time.

You ask your customers, as discussed in Chapter 1. And you ask the people on the receiving end of what you do, the people you count on for results. You construct reality as they see it. You face the challenges as they understand them, bringing into clear view what stands in the way of improvement.

21

Why People Don't Do What You Ask

Asking those on the receiving end of your training and motivation efforts how they see their world is a very direct way to find out what stands in the way of the behaviors you need. Human performance improvement can be made a very complex subject. Or it can be made very simple and practical.

When efforts to enhance productivity fall short, there may be many reasons, but most of the time, it is one of the following three:

1. People don't know what you expect or why you expect it, which is a matter of management direction.
2. They don't know how to do what you want, which depends upon knowledge, skill, and job aids.
3. They don't believe the achievement is worth the price that must be paid in extra effort, which boils down to motivation.

Planning with a sense of vision and scope helps you give proper, simultaneous attention to all three issues and to face up to the very real human constraints to change.

A Disturbing Reticence

In business today, we find major companies wanting to change but not getting as far as they want as fast as they want. A lot of key players who have the ability to make a difference are sitting on the sidelines frustrated and immobilized.

The takeover game, restructuring, and the shrinking of staffs have had a devastating effect on employee commitment and loyalty, especially within the ranks of middle managers. Top managers, too, have their own change-induced problems. They are beset by what they view as the short-term demands of both parent companies and Wall Street, and the atmosphere of takeover mania puts them under pressure to do damage to their companies in order to save them.

Workers and managers at every level of American business sense something is drastically wrong. Many are unhappy in their work and irritated with their organizations. They complain about poor communication, irrelevant training, distant and aloof management, and a widening gap between what companies say they stand for and day-to-day reality.

Salving the Pain of Change

For many, change is a painful thing. The late Eric Hoffer, a real worker's philosopher, addresses the pain of change in his book *The Ordeal of Change*. As a young man in the Great Depression, Hoffer worked the farmlands of California as a day laborer. He had gotten used to picking lettuce, which took some time to learn to do well. One day he learned that his crew would be moved off the next day to pick peas. He was up half the night worrying about how he would go about it, wondering if he would be able to do a good job.

There is a lot of pain for people when they try to change from something familiar to something new and different. Managers often fail to appreciate that people who have not accepted or "bought into" the vision will continue to see things as they are, not as they are going to be.

A construction site, for example, is a mess of destruction for a while, but that's the reason for the architect's sketch. It portrays the vision of the fine new facility that will emerge from the chaos.

That's important, because a lot of people get frustrated by upheaval. They need to be reminded that changes in method are the business parallel to all the banging, clanging, dirt, and confusion of a construction site, something worth going through to accomplish something better.

The "People Solution": Eliciting Human Commitment

Forging a partnership for greater productivity starts with challenge, because unless there is intense craving for something better, the price of vast change will not be paid.

People costs run to an average of about 70 percent in American businesses today. Very little of that figure goes toward manufacturing labor costs. The bulk of it goes to people who are designing and selling products and services, and to the people who support and sustain their efforts. These are tasks for which it is unlikely a machine or computer will ever be invented. The fact is, business has never been more people-driven, and wide-scale change cannot happen without large numbers of people participating and working in unison. In today's business environment, there needs to be a "Declaration of Interdependence." The solitary business performer is as obsolete as the frontier cowboy.

Assess Organizational Values

The value system of an organization is critical to what the organization will accomplish. The analysis of internal beliefs is sometimes considered to be the soft, mushy part of business planning, to be skipped or abridged. But it is a very important foundation step to understand how your organizational audiences think, what they believe is important, and how they differ from each other as individuals, depending upon their unique life experiences. It is important to serve up what you are asking in ways congruent with those beliefs. If you need fresh perspectives from the people you are counting on, you need to work at creating receptivity to such changes.

When General Motors restructured into Super Groups, each containing several automobile divisions, introducing significant cultural as well as business change, the first major conference of all the stakeholders was given the theme "Day One." Event locations included the soaring halls of a major art museum to create an environment of creativity, to open minds to the drama of the change process.

As dedicated individuals were thrown into the mixmaster of new responsibilities and challenges in an entire new landscape of how business would be conducted, the same questions were expressed time and time again, publicly and privately:

- "Do they mean it?" ("They" referring to whoever did the rearranging. "It" referring to such stated goals as decentralized decision making.)
- "What does this mean to me personally? Where do I fit?" The key here is "I." The world is made up of individuals.

The theme here is that business performance is tied directly to human performance. Both require simultaneous improvement if we are to entertain the hope of being world-class competitors. By and large, many managers recognize that change can provide opportunities. Like the Chinese, who see in "crisis" and "opportunity" the very same word, they have learned how to set corporate goals and to strategize total business planning, at least on paper. But many have not yet figured out how to focus total organizational power behind change.

Business leaders cannot create success with sound plans and imaginative strategies alone. The traditional emphasis on modern plant and equipment, product development, control systems, and sales aggressiveness are sound actions, but they can produce only anemic results unless an equally intense effort is made to forge work force commitment and improve the performance of people on the job.

Human habits and perceptions, turf conflicts, network ties, and personal fears all complicate the process, as do confusing information with communication, and meetings and messages with teaching.

The Importance of Building Trust

Partnerships depend upon building trust. This is more than communicating clearly so that "they" understand "you." It is vital that "you" understand "them"—that you comprehend the hopes, fears, and problems of those you want to reach.

You need to convey in tone, manner, and action that you are drawing up a realistic, people-centered assessment, not as an exercise or a report, but as the front end of serious and sustained performance improvement. You will be taking the time to put into place what significant change must have—intangibles that are too often overlooked like:

- Credibility—You mean what you say and say what you mean.
- Confidence—You know what to do.
- Consistency—You are working from a longer run assessment, not a whim of the moment.
- Context—You can show how separate actions fit together.

Trust, and education to create the understandings upon which trust is based, are at the heart of a strategy of partnerships.

Overcoming Work Force Cynicism

Russell Baker, in one of his humorous columns, fantasizes about living in "Adland." In Adland, he satirically explains, airplanes run on time, stores give excellent service, and everything works like it's supposed to.

Just as the public knows that businesses do not always measure up to the promises they make in their advertising, so within organizations, staffs perceive a widening gap between what the organization proclaims via meetings, banners, and video reports, and what the organization truly expects of them.

The process of drawing up a realistic situational assessment depends upon the quality and depth of the questions you ask. Superficial questions will yield superficial answers. Search out the cynics. This is time to hear the mavericks out. When you design meetings and training sessions, don't just sit back and admire your handiwork. Watch the audience watching the event. Body language will tell you a lot. Invariably, the best place to view the proceedings is near the door where the cynics gather, poised between staying and leaving.

Today's work force is better educated than ever and has high expectations. There is diminished loyalty to the organization. Workers do not listen to or follow others just because they are bosses. They pay attention to the authority of competence.

People have to understand the mission if they are going to invest their confidence in it. Otherwise, they worry, obstruct, or become neutral, passive spectators. Few organizations, not even the biggest, are powerful enough to move forward vigorously with that kind of wind drag. The work force that grows increasingly intelligent and cynical understands the difference between a crusade and a charade and commits itself accordingly.

Analyze How People Learn and Get Information

For your performance improvement assessment, it is important to inventory how your people get their information and their learning, and how new time-saving, cost-saving routes into the mind are being developed rapidly. How those methods are being used, or misused, is a very important matter to understand these days.

As computers, desktop publishing, low-cost video, and other tools proliferate, they can be misapplied to simply add to the information glut. They are frequently used randomly as part of fragmented activities rather than as integrated weapons in tight linkage with mainstream corporate objectives. Yet looked at creatively and strategically, the technologies of learning today are far ahead of the imagination of users to apply their capabilities.

Conclusion: Let's Build Ships

There are no villains out there—not foreigners, bosses, unions, or customers. It's just a new and different business world.

Organizations are hungry for change. They have talented and capable leaders to lead the charge. The issue is not willingness. The issue is channeling that energy so that people start to see progress and sample small victories.

But the corporate complexities, the turf issues, the changing values of the work force, and the misuse of powerful linkages of communication all combine to frustrate the best-intentioned efforts. Task forces meet, business plans get hammered out, consultants leave their reports, new directions are communicated, and feverish activity ensues. Then, looking back, very little of true strategic import, of true marketplace advantage, of true relevance to the customer emerges from the commotion. The dust settles and the costly cycle of futility begins anew.

The idea of total business strategy—a total strategy that factors in human performance—is important to emphasize as the most practical way to achieve and sustain a marketplace-visible margin of difference.

Consider the question: "If you were marooned on an island and could have just one book, what would it be?" There are lots of possible answers, ranging from inspirational books to the world's great novels. The answer I prefer is *Morton's Book of Practical Shipbuilding*.

Mobilizing people means building vessels, crafting solutions that people you are counting on understand as connected to the real-world issues they face and capable of making their lives better.

Using challenge constructively is the way to build ships that can take your organization from where you are to where you want to be.

Checklist for Change

☑ Ask those you count on how they see the situation, to help you know and to create receptivity for change.

☑ Assess organizational values; pinpoint human constraints to change.

☑ Analyze the causes of work force cynicism and take measures to alleviate them.

☑ Inventory how your people currently learn and receive information in this data-abundant world.

☑ Round out your situational assessment with your business plan objectives. Put those goals to the tests of external reality and the capability of your people to carry out those objectives.

Apply the Learning

List your five biggest areas of challenge or high payout improvement. Be specific about what various people need to do more of, less of, or differently to have an impact on results.

3

Scale Your Thinking to the Magnitude of Your Problems

Make no little plans. They have no power to
stir the blood.   DANIEL BURNHAM

Make No Little Plans

To Daniel Burnham, "make no little plans" was not just a motto. He was
the visionary architect of the plan to create a magnificent waterfront for
the city of Chicago.

To mobilize people into productivity partnerships, it's important that
there be sufficient scale and dimension to your thinking because most
crusades for change accumulate their power and credibility or their
weakness and futility at the very beginning.

In a world of global competition, with governments and entire industries strategizing their attacks on each other's markets, the story of
David beating Goliath is a rousing but inappropriate tale. Subscribing to
such legends is causing some organizations and managers to have the
twentieth-century equivalent of slingshots rammed right down their
throats.

Organizations today are increasingly complex, interdependent, and multileveled. Functions have often been added in an unrationalized manner so that there are overlapping charters and turf conflicts. Organizations seeking to get their people moving can find their troops deployed over millions of square miles of territory. The problems of distance are compounded when the people being mobilized are franchise holders or suppliers who act only when the initiatives are clearly in their self-interest.

Developing solutions that truly equate to the size and persistence of the challenges is important in any phase of a business. If you decide to take a trip from New York to Paris and then scale back the effort and funding to 75 percent as good enough, you end up in Iceland.

When it comes to mobilizing people, efforts of scale and power are particularly important. People routinely transport their bodies to the workplace, but they hold back their commitments of mind and spirit until they have confidence that the missions are truly achievable. Too many organizations and too many managers are "ending up in Iceland" without understanding that the seeds of the shortfall were set by the narrow scope of their original thinking.

The first two chapters started with steps that help you assess the situations you face. The chapter that follows this one takes up how to develop frameworks for moving from a business plan to a performance plan. This chapter examines interpretive skills and attitudes that help you look at today and tomorrow from a number of angles so that you see the full implications and can turn the corner to sustainable action. The interpretive perspectives include:

1. Envisioning the kind of future you want so clearly that you can describe this better tomorrow with fervor

2. Focusing on organizational interconnections, how the various levels and disciplines fit together

3. Visualizing time—the weeks, months, years ahead—so that a rhythm of accomplishment can be developed

4. Concentrating on solutions, not "stuff"; on answers, not activities; on results, not rhetoric

5. Guiding the thinking process smoothly from vision and scope to simple execution, funneling down to the best and most practical ideas

Visioneering:
An Indispensable Skill
for the Nineties

Vision Is a Precious Resource

At a birthday party in the early 1930s, David Sarnoff, the young president of RCA, thanked his friends and colleagues for the presents they had given him.

"But you know what I really want?" he asked. And then he described the concept we now call television.

David Sarnoff had a vision. He shared it. His talented associates understood it and believed in it. Several years later, they gave Sarnoff what he really wanted.

Vision is seeing the possibilities—not just where you are but where you want to be. From a human-performance perspective, it is something to be shared, explained, and emotionalized, in the name of getting others to help make it happen.

When organizing for major change, leaders need to see clearly the future point at which the world will be better for themselves and the people they lead. Visioneering is the ability to see this future point so cogently that you can describe it.

A practical exercise to help individuals or teams articulate their vision is for them to compose an article for the major trade publication of their field or industry, describing the company at a future point in time. The exercise gets individuals really thinking and feeling what this better world will be like. The act of describing what you want to become has the potential to stimulate involvement and the setting of realistic expectations, underscoring what we are working to achieve rather than prematurely claiming accomplishment.

Volatility Makes Vision Essential

When business was less volatile, most executives didn't need to spend a lot of time visioneering. Banks were banks. Cars were cars. Hotels were hotels. It was possible to go through an entire business career without ever having to envision or prepare for a dramatically different kind of business.

But turbulence in the marketplace and the pace of innovation are rendering that picture obsolete. Cars, for example, are transportation, and, at the same time, they compete for recreation dollars. Banks have become big retailers, not just of money, but of all kinds of investments. Many hotels are packaged resort and/or conference centers. These kinds of business upheavals, in which entire industries begin to overlap, confuse not only customers but the work force as well.

In reviewing the initial draft of his first major address as the president of General Motors, Jim McDonald put it this way, "I don't care about words, those can be polished later. Let's talk core concepts." As McDonald became more comfortable with his awesome operating responsibilities and more frustrated by the upheavals in the automobile industry and the constraints of an organization the size of General Motors, he came to recognize more fully the importance of using his office to set thematic direction. For example, McDonald's "new quality ethic" dramatically expressed organizational values and priorities regarding product quality improvements, forcefully articulating the forward directions, but leaving others to fill in the tactics.

Communicating the Vision

Until fairly recently, executives who did have a vision and shared it in the boardroom could reasonably expect the organization to pick up and move in the proper direction. But executives are finding that doesn't happen automatically anymore, especially in big organizations built like 19th-century autocracies. Directions are missed, garbled, or ignored. Sometimes the message gets out all right, but there's confusion over who should do what, when, and how.

The result? Diminished energy, reduced performance levels, and lack of momentum.

Today, research can measure not only beliefs but the intensity of those beliefs. When you are counting on your staff to do a lot more or a lot different than you have ever asked, it is an important foundational step to increase that intensity of belief, to mount crusades of change rather than simply alter methods or procedures.

A vivid description of where you are going is important capital for organizational leaders. It can be one of the most powerful parts of learning and communication agendas. When you discuss today's business matters, you rarely have superior insights or fresh information. The assessments of subordinates regarding today's business are sometimes superior to their bosses', since the subordinates are closer to the firing line. So future direction is the area where leaders can make their greatest contribution.

Presenting the vision isn't just to create understanding or belief, but to increase the intensity of belief.

"Visionaphobia"

Business leaders sometimes are squeamish about vision. They see it as inconsequential, private, or otherworldly. Some may choose not to share their vision because they fear the possibility of falling short. They want to maintain the flexibility to say that whatever has been accomplished is what they had in mind. That's like the boy shooting at a fence. A passing stranger noticed the hole was always smack in the bull's eye. "Not hard," the youngster explained. "First I shoot, then I draw the bull's eye around the hole." But in preserving such flexibility, leaders pass up one of the most powerful drivers of serious change.

Jeanne Kirkpatrick understands the power of vision and ideas. As the U.S. ambassador to the United Nations, she would not let an argument of ideology go unchallenged. To her, these were not just words. As she put it, "Ideas have consequences." An example of the power of ideas is the opening of the Berlin Wall. As the first joyful East Germans poured through, some noticed a prophecy that had been crudely spray-painted on the wall several years before: "This wall will fall. Beliefs become reality." Ideas shaped with clarity have the power to ignite action. Whoever conveys the most compelling vision of the future has the best chance of earning the involvement of the people who must carry it out.

Utilizing the Political Model

People in politics understand well the value of vision. President John Kennedy's idea of putting an American on the moon in the 1960s, the "Great Society" social legislation of President Lyndon Johnson, Martin Luther King's "I Have a Dream" speech—all were visions that caught the public's attention and galvanized the power to make things happen.

These leaders understood how to get people excited about possibilities. And they gave their audiences the feel and the taste for a specific achievement. They painted a picture of what could be and dramatized it.

Politicians become quite good at creating thematic vision because their followers regularly vote on whether they ought to stay in office. Observe the rigors of a major election and you will see the themes continually sharpened and honed. Commenting on the failure of his party to win the White House, Bruce Babbitt, governor of Arizona, said, "Our party wiped away the graffiti of the past, but we didn't paint a mural of the future."

Visioneering Is Disciplined Work

Visioneering is hard work. It is not just lofty words or chart pages stuck up around the wall of an off-site meeting. If not crafted in a tough, disciplined way, vision and mission statements can become overgeneralized wish lists. A vision of the future should not be simply what you want to accomplish, but should include what you and your people must contribute to make the future you envision feasible.

"And It's Worth Getting Emotional About"

There are dimensions of history, drama, philosophy, even poetry in the battles being fought today by business. Business creates jobs. Business wins and keeps customers by providing value. Business is filled with quiet heroes. Too many organizations try to get major improvements without painting the vision that can tap the emotional, visceral side of change. Watch people cheering at a ball game, which in the larger scheme of things means very little. Watch them make heroes out of athletes who often have nowhere near the courage of quiet, anonymous people trying to drag their companies into a changed future. There is a craving in our world for meaning. The vision of what an organization is trying to accomplish can help provide that meaning.

The magic of vision is that it offers a way to involve and inspire people, to get them to want to go to a new place. The value of vision in moving great numbers of people is proven time and time again in politics, in the military, in theology, as well as in business. In striving for human-performance gains, it's worth taking the time and energy to paint the picture of a better world.

...And it's worth getting emotional about.

From Vision to Scope

To scope is to gain an integrative vision of the entire picture. It's seeing the pieces and the parts and how they fit together: the product, the producer, the service, the customer, the competition, the market, here and down the line, simultaneously, all of it, together, in context.

Avoid the Seductiveness of Shortcuts

The "Symptoms" Plague. Managers get paid to do many things. According to textbook theories, they are there to plan, organize, control, and lead. In reality, managers spend most of their time putting out brush-fire problems.

The phone rings at all the worst possible times to explain that, "we have a problem down here in the warehouse," or "Arlene called in sick, and there's nobody around who can generate the printouts we need for this afternoon's board meeting." Being a successful firefighter is considered "just part of the job" these days.

Assaulting the wrong targets with vigor has become a common failing in companies today. It reflects, perhaps, the American impetuousness to act first and ask questions later—sort of ready, fire, aim. It would be easy to conclude that philosopher George Santayana had just come from a modern business huddle when he ironically observed, "Fanaticism consists in redoubling your efforts when you have forgotten your aim." The prevailing tendency is to look at company situations much too narrowly—as though everything else in the business is detached and static. The predictable result of this small-bore analysis is repetitive problems, frustration, and higher costs.

The Instant-Gratification, Quick-Fix Mentality. American families leave the television set on for an average of 6 hours a day. Channels are changed an average of 34 times each day in the typical home. The experience since early childhood of watching dozens of sitcoms and hundreds of commercials a week has led many workers to expect simple answers and immediate solutions. The accumulated experience of such instant gratification has now moved into some aspects of business decision making.

How does this quick-fix mentality happen in the best of companies? Such shortcuts are tempting to managers who take one small piece of a situation and jump to the conclusion that they have a fully dimensioned assessment. Such managers find their people do not go into gear because they believe, rightly, that this is just one more flurry, unanchored to a coherent view of where the business must move.

A Room with a View, or Seeing the Big Picture

See the Entire Organization. A fully dimensioned view of the situations you face requires a multilevel view of your own organization. Large and complex organizations are vulnerable to developing performance improvement efforts that are inconsistent and at times contain contradictions.

The responsibilities for informing, communicating, teaching, coaching, evaluating, and rewarding tend to be haphazardly distributed among a number of functions in many organizations. If the executives responsible for profit results, business planning, marketing, management information systems, human resource planning, training, meetings and events, company newspapers, executive video reports, appraisal and compensation mechanisms, and many other influences on people do not coordinate their efforts, then the sorting is left to those on the receiving end.

Develop Harmony Between Elements. You need to look at the organization holistically because that is the only way you will get a harmony between elements. Serious, sustained, organizational improvement requires a unity between:

- What's operationally important, what will make a difference in your marketplace.
- How you hire against those requirements.
- How you teach the true success factors.
- How you measure and reward what happens.

Lining up these elements may seem tantalizingly easy, but it's as difficult as getting the four cherries in a row in the Las Vegas slot machines to create the big jackpot payoff. In too many organizations these days, these key elements never quite get lined up.

Once you have a clear view of the organization in terms of its levels and functional interconnections, you need to move next to a clear, dimensional view of time.

Strategizing for Results over Time

Building Fences Behind Incremental Gains. Creating receptivity for improvement takes time. Business leaders must provide time for learning to be internalized. This means allowing time for experimental applications of innovative ideas and for small victories that reinforce the learning process. It also means devoting attention to the optimum timing for such stimuli as meetings, courses, new initiatives, and incentives. The objective is to simultaneously create a sense of momentum and a rhythm of accomplishment. Do too much and people become overwhelmed. Do too little and the sense of priority and mission dissipates.

Strategizing the use of time encourages patience. In most carefully targeted organizational improvement situations, significant results can be accomplished over time. Too many serious and productive efforts are aborted because they don't achieve immediate results. Each abort lessens the credibility of subsequent efforts.

As head of the United Automobile Workers, Walter Reuther achieved big gains for his constituents. He used contract negotiation milestones to earn conceptual breakthroughs. In achieving cost of living adjustments and guaranteed annual wages, he sold his initiatives by taking a longer time perspective. He was content to have those breakthroughs get underway with very modest costs. Once the principles were established and the mechanisms put into place, costs escalated rapidly at subsequent contract bargaining points, a strategy that could only be initiated by someone taking a longer time horizon.

It's smart to space out the efforts, give people a chance to sample new experiences and get comfortable. You can do this when you use a longer time horizon.

Moving Agendas. Lloyd Reuss, executive vice president in charge of North American Automotive Operations for General Motors, likes to think in terms of "moving agendas." A serious student of organizational communications strategy, Reuss prefers to avoid addressing a number of topics at once, instead focusing on one topic in particular, discussing that topic at a number of levels in the organization over a carefully thought-through time frame, until the issues are well understood and people start to behave differently. He then moves on to the next major issue so that his communications take on the added impact of signaling total organizational focus. "There's no point," he counsels, "in talking about everything to everybody all at once."

Begin at the End. Start by thinking of what you want people to do. Then consider what skills, knowledge, and attitudes need to be in place to accomplish this. Follow up by asking yourself what master performers, in your organization or in other companies that you respect, do better and differently.

Don't dabble. If you can't make something better, leave it alone. There are periods when the best action is inaction, when the organization needs time to integrate earlier initiatives. When you move, do so with power, force, and focus. Develop the reputation that when you are involved, the magnitude and power of the solution will match the scale, intensity, and pervasiveness of the problem.

Move from Scope to Simplicity

There is a funny and famous quote from Mark Twain which sums it up well: "I am sorry I had to write you such a long letter. I didn't have time to write you a short one."

The issue is this: How do you scope out a problem, then simplify it, so that it makes sense to people who can do something to solve it?

In organizational communication and performance improvement, distilling ideas and concepts to their essentials is an important step. Less is more. Complexity and information overload are enemies of real change. The most fundamental mistake that well-intentioned corporations make when they get serious about performance improvement is to measure progress by volume, pages, pictures, and other "stuff." It is essential to keep the focus on solutions, not stuff, on results rather than activities, on what is being done rather than what is being shipped out to users. The way for all the stakeholders in the change process to think of scope and simplicity is not as opposites or enemies but as two steps in a strategic process—one addressing the need to define the real problem in all of its dimensions, the second breaking down the problem into achievable components that human beings can do something about.

Keeping things simple so that employees and colleagues understand involves more than simplicity of language. It is essential as well to keep the work proportioned to the discipline of time.

With the proliferation of information, time, as a finite resource, becomes the great leveler. Performance-improvement initiatives have to be understood and carried out by people who, no matter how affluent materially, face a new kind of impoverishment: time poverty. Despite how much there is to be accomplished, the sun rises and sets in the same ancient, disciplined rhythms. So while performance-improvement initiatives may be sophisticated in design, they need to be expressed in simple, practical ways for people who are short of time.

Sound Creative Process

As Figure 3-1 illustrates, moving from scope to simplicity can be considered a kind of funneling process. In strategic planning, you start by considering the widest range of possibilities. Next you narrow the alternatives down to answer the practical question: What do we do about it? Finally, you need to move the process along and funnel it into disciplined, practical actions.

Creative thinking starts with bold and wide-ranging alternatives. The process calls for brainstorming and bold "what if" thinking. The most

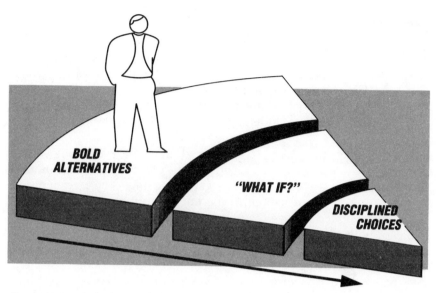

Figure 3-1. Move from scope to simplicity.

important breakthroughs can emerge at this stage. The point is to get everything out on the table. Only then does the assessing of alternatives—the simplifying and selection phase—begin.

As an example, consider how dreadfully complex national defense is in the current nuclear age. Experts spend entire careers exploring possibilities and alternatives like the Strategic Defense Initiative. That's scope. Then, to sell the concept to Congress and the people, President Reagan comes along and narrows all this complex business down to something he calls "Star Wars." That's simplicity.

Similarly, the creators of the classic TV learning program *Sesame Street* use the process to combine education and entertainment for a very tough audience. Educators establish the learning goals: teach the alphabet, teach the numbers, teach how to tie a shoe. But the entertainers come in and rightly understand that unless they can make the lessons fun, the kids will be bored stiff. So clever cartooning, music, and youthful humor custom-designed for educating that age group are brought into the mix.

If this process is important for children, it applies even more with adults, who carry into organizational functions and programs a lifetime of learning and experience and who open their minds guardedly to what they find useful, practical, and relevant to the issues they face every day.

Layer Information

Once asked about a basic formula, physicist Albert Einstein replied without apology that he didn't know the formula. That surprised some listeners until he explained further, "I don't fill my mind with information I can find anytime I want it."

Similarly, law schools don't teach laws, because laws continually change. They teach law students how to analyze and think, and where to look up what they need when they need it.

Many business people try to tell everything about everything, which complicates and often confuses matters. But the great need in communications today is for less, not more—a weeding out of the extraneous so people can act on information. In this era of information overload and communication technology that gives on-demand retrieval, the requirements of both scope and simplicity can be combined by the layering of information. Think through what should go into the mind, such as concepts and patterns of performance. Consider what is better placed at the fingertips, such as information and job aids. The best approach is to communicate only as much as is necessary and put elaborations and details in some sort of addendum.

Kerchunking

Kerchunking is the answer to the riddle "How do you eat an elephant?" The answer, of course, is to cut it up into thousands of bite-size pieces first.

Magnitude sometimes intimidates people. Missions seem to become too big, too complex, too difficult. It is useful to break the big idea down into manageable segments, into smaller pieces that individuals can do something about.

One continuing issue is how far out in time to project a vision. Nearer and specific has proven superior to far-out and generalized. Rhetoric alone won't move people for long. They need reinforcement through winning small victories.

Breaking the Code

When you think of scope and simplicity as a creative continuum, it can help you break the code, that is, better understand the differences that can arise between partners in change. Many times, what seems like disagreement is no more than individuals using different vocabularies or being at different points in the developmental continuum.

The ability to break the code and reconcile seeming differences is especially important in forging partnerships for productivity. Today, the partners in a team effort often represent forces that see matters from different perspectives, like unions and management, purchasers and suppliers, or headquarters and field staffers. It can be especially damaging when consortiums for change get sidetracked by the inability to reconcile scope and simplicity, by impatience with different vocabularies and thinking patterns.

Consider, for example, the counterproductive potential in being caught in a blazing cross fire between two executives, both smart, tough-minded decision makers, but with quite different backgrounds. One is sophisticated and classically educated, with a doctorate in marketing and a string of world-class credentials. At the same level in the organization is an operating executive who prides himself on his street savvy. You're getting directions from both sides, solutions have to be approved by each, and these men don't always communicate well with each other.

This kind of political infighting could be a recipe for confusion and paralysis, with people falling into the trap of taking sides. One executive represented sophisticated scope, the other represented real-world practicality—scope and simplicity.

The two styles can be combined to advantage. The answer in such a tug-of-war is not to go one way or the other, depending on who happens to be more forceful. It was clear what each wanted. Both executives really had the same goals: to sell more products and satisfy customers. But their vocabularies were different, reflecting their different backgrounds. Once the code was broken, it became possible to design solutions that represented the best of each set of perspectives, a perfect marriage of scope and simplicity. The mix became more powerful than the separate ingredients.

Conclusion: Wintertime Bridges

The winters in my home state of Michigan can be long and severe. When engineers design roofs or bridges, they have to build into them the extra capacity to carry heavy snow loads and the stress that comes with freezing and thawing. The same thinking should apply to your business plans. Business is in for a period of heavy weather, not a time to base plans and strategies on wooden stilts. Business leaders need to recognize the magnitude of their challenges and meet them with strategies of equal scale.

We emphasize early deliberations on the appropriate magnitude of effort because you rarely achieve more than you expect. We need wintertime bridges that not only look good but stand up to the rigors of real-world use.

When you look at your organization from a number of perspectives simultaneously, you embolden and sharpen your thinking. When you think about problems and situations through the eyes of your customer, you focus on how your company earns its profit. When you see your organization holistically, all of the echelons and intersects, you think about how to get all the forces moving in the same direction. When you propel yourself out to a distant point in time, you think not only about where you are going, but about competitive actions as well. When you can move from a wide-sweeping assessment and start to sharpen the focus to simple, practical actions, you are ready to start developing a framework for action, a performance plan.

Checklist for Change

☑ Scale your thinking so that the magnitude of the solution matches the size and persistence of the problem.

☑ Focus on solutions, not "stuff"; answers, not activities; results, not rhetoric.

☑ See the organizational interconnections, eliminate contradictions in messages.

☑ Develop a harmony between what's important and how you hire, teach, measure, and reward.

☑ Use time strategically to space out events and develop a rhythm of accomplishment.

☑ Use "moving agendas," focusing on key issues until you see change and then moving on.

☑ Describe your vision to create understanding and increase the intensity of belief.

☑ Proportion efforts to the constraints of time—put information into layers. Decide what people should learn and what they can retrieve when they need it.

☑ Combine scope of vision with simplicity of execution.

Apply the Learning

Engage in a bold "what if?" exercise. Take your biggest business problem and let your mind wander to what it would really take, by you and others you count on, for that problem to go away forever.

4
Construct
a Framework
for Action

If you do not know where you're going, any
road will get you there.　　ANONYMOUS

A Simply Designed,
Agreed-Upon, Visible
Playbook

Professional football teams use "playbooks" so each member can learn exactly what to do when the quarterback calls a particular play. The book assigns each player a role, shows where each fits into the total play, and synchronizes individual efforts into team performance.

The way a pro football team drives forward with power and efficiency when a set of numbers is called, is quite a bit different from youngsters playing the same game. At a typical playground, the quarterback says something like, "Alex, you run out for a pass by the garbage cans. Jessie, you go over by the car just in case." As the huddle breaks up, Alex turns and asks, "Which cans, the small ones or the big ones?"

It's astonishing how many companies run the people phases of their business as loosely as the way kids play sandlot football. Everybody knows the object is to score, of course, but they don't know how it's to be done, who does what, or precisely where they fit. So on an intricate play, when it's time to hand off, nobody is there. Confidence erodes. Plays are simplified, so the business becomes predictable to competition and boring to customers. The organization doesn't hit with the force with which it is capable. Worst of all, the very game you are playing becomes so disjointed and vaguely focused that it's like a sports team entering the field wielding baseball bats, basketballs, footballs, and lacrosse sticks. As the game unfolds, the shortstop, pivoting to complete a key play, gets sacked by a fellow player streaking in from left field. The first baseman, incensed by the left fielder's poor judgment, retaliates by rapping the quarterback across the shins with his lacrosse stick. Then a free-for-all breaks loose.

Sure, the outside world is chaotic and unpredictable, but that's even more reason to keep confusion out of the locker room and the workplace. Whether it's sports or the far tougher game of business, the object is not to thrive on chaos, but to avoid it. How does this confusion happen? Ask yourself: Where is the simply designed, agreed-upon playbook?

Managers and workers throughout the company have titles and functions, of course, but they do not know how to approach the specific tasks at hand. And so the pace of improvement actions gets bogged down in long-winded conversations.

What's going on is that in today's complex organizations, human beings carry frameworks around in their heads, constructs of how to look at various situations, how to solve problems, how to achieve improvement. For small-gauge improvements, simple operations, tiny staffs who know each other well or professionals who share similar education, visible frameworks of change don't have to be put on the table in a literal, tangible way. But for complex, interdependent organizations, it is very important to visualize a shared framework for action.

Diagram the Process

So that improvement becomes and remains dynamic and systemic, it is useful to diagram the improvement process, showing participants where they are, where they are going, the steps needed to get there, and how lessons learned feed back into the process. By diagraming it, you show the skeleton, which is easier for participants to refer to than words. The diagram shows how to move from concept to action to measurement.

A framework can be thought of as a map, a playbook, a path of accomplishment to provide teams of people with a common frame of reference—sort of a "yellow brick road." The framework opens up the strategic process and invites all players to share in it. In a very practical way, the framework organizes and categorizes people's time and talents and sets them against tasks and results.

Use Systems Techniques

The kind of systems thinking that is widely used in the space program, high-tech product development, and construction also has valuable applications to human resources issues. The transferability is readily apparent to some. Others need a graphic demonstration.

I recently attended a seminar which turned into a debate on this very subject. One old-line cynic listened awhile and then loudly proclaimed the new approach to be a bunch of fancy hogwash. He said anybody with a head on his shoulders and common sense didn't need all the rigamarole of a systems approach.

Unfazed, the systems proponent asked, "Do you work alone or with a lot of other people?"

The man replied that he worked with other people in a large corporation.

"Well," the systems enthusiast replied, "you're right. Everybody carries ideas and experiences around in their heads. But their background seldom matches what's in somebody else's head, so you have to spend a lot of time straightening people out, discussing what you mean, where you are, what you're trying to accomplish. Right?"

"Right," the critic agreed grudgingly, but you could see a glimmer of understanding.

Too many companies initiate major change without developing an integrative improvement system and then diagraming the process so that all the stakeholders understand the plan.

Most companies have no frameworks. People go to meetings. They talk. But nobody says what the real point or the destination is. It's just repetitive chatter, because everybody is coming from somewhere different, and they run into problems trying to figure out how to get to another place together. The process is draining because the people involved don't even use the same vocabularies, and they don't share the knowledge of a common framework.

Working without a framework renders building fences behind decisions virtually impossible. Consequently, the next cycle revisits the same ground as the previous one.

Examples of Frameworks

Figure 4-1 shows a model for diagraming the overall process of performance development. It is an upside-down triangle, with the customer at

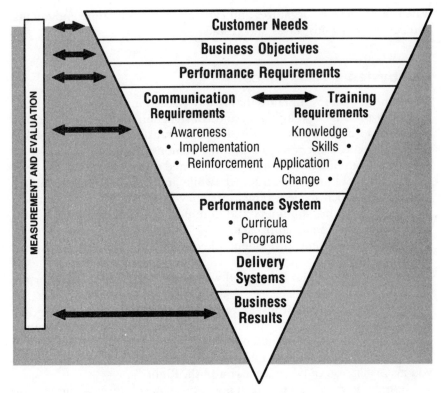

Figure 4-1. A performance improvement model. (*Courtesy of Sandy Corporation*).

the top, illustrating that customer needs ought to drive most developmental activities. This, then, breaks the key steps down into business objectives, performance requirements, communication requirements, training requirements, performance system curricula and programs, delivery systems, and measurement and evaluation of business results.

Diagraming clarifies thinking and is even more valuable when tailored to specific industries. Figures 4-2 and 4-3 show two variations of a systems diagram, one for franchisees in the auto industry, the other for a major hotel chain.

Allow Latitude for Variation

Good systems planning avoids tying individual entrepreneurs within an organizational setting into lockstep decisions. Common to virtually all successful business executives is that they think through how they want

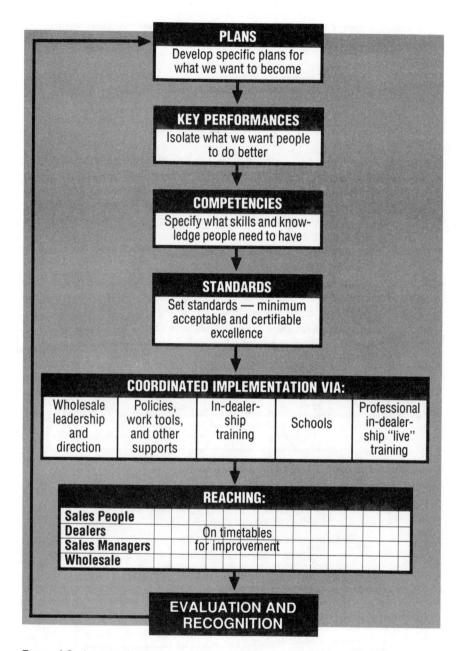

Figure 4-2. An example of a framework for performance improvement used by independent franchise holders in the automotive industry. (*Courtesy of Chevrolet Motor Division.*)

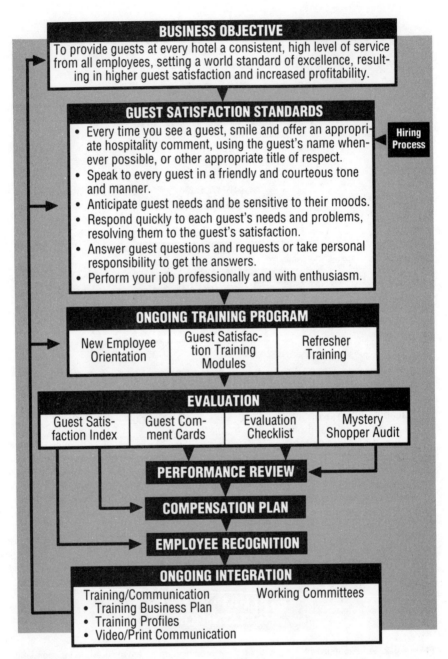

BUSINESS OBJECTIVE

To provide guests at every hotel a consistent, high level of service from all employees, setting a world standard of excellence, resulting in higher guest satisfaction and increased profitability.

GUEST SATISFACTION STANDARDS

- Every time you see a guest, smile and offer an appropriate hospitality comment, using the guest's name whenever possible, or other appropriate title of respect.
- Speak to every guest in a friendly and courteous tone and manner.
- Anticipate guest needs and be sensitive to their moods.
- Respond quickly to each guest's needs and problems, resolving them to the guest's satisfaction.
- Answer guest questions and requests or take personal responsibility to get the answers.
- Perform your job professionally and with enthusiasm.

Hiring Process

ONGOING TRAINING PROGRAM

New Employee Orientation	Guest Satisfaction Training Modules	Refresher Training

EVALUATION

Guest Satisfaction Index	Guest Comment Cards	Evaluation Checklist	Mystery Shopper Audit

PERFORMANCE REVIEW

COMPENSATION PLAN

EMPLOYEE RECOGNITION

ONGOING INTEGRATION

Training/Communication   Working Committees
- Training Business Plan
- Training Profiles
- Video/Print Communication

Figure 4-3. A guest satisfaction system model.   (*Courtesy of ITT Sheraton Corporation.*)

things done. However, their conclusions might be quite different from their colleagues and counterparts in other parts of the country. Indeed, regional and personality differences should be factored into the framework as variables. Systemic process has the advantage of encouraging rather than retarding this kind of individualization. The systems approach and the diagramed framework show the path and the principles. Individual business people who vary the practices learn to do so in a knowledgeable way.

More Participation, Less Frustration

Another key advantage of frameworks is that they make the process of getting from here to there participative. People are not likely to feel left out or useless when they can see a process in its entirety and their special place in it.

When the improvement path is clear and widely published, it shows people how to cut into the decision-making framework, how to talk to their bosses, how to serve up their recommendations in some kind of context, and how to merge their ideas with the good ideas of colleagues.

When the path is clear and consistent, it reduces frustration. Anyone who has ever driven an automobile in a strange city with a passenger giving directions a block at a time knows the feeling. You have no idea whether your destination is two blocks or twenty miles away. By doling out directions a little bit at a time, your companion is exerting a form of information control. It's a far better feeling when somebody has plotted out the entire trip in advance. Then, specific directions to turn right or left have contextual meaning and are useful reminders.

With a framework in place, the total trip is broken down—where you start, where you turn, which direction you turn, where the barriers are, how to get around them. A framework lets you know where the changes are likely to occur and gives you a chance to celebrate milestones of achievement.

Maintain Process Integrity

An additional benefit of frameworks is that they help maintain the integrity of processes. Managers of manufacturing plants will tell you that their biggest problem is not *achieving* a given quality level but *maintaining* it. People regularly achieve some acceptable level of manufacturing quality, but each day, variations in the process accumulate until the entire process is bent out of shape. Quality falls off again because there is no documentation of exactly how it was attained the first go-around.

A framework shows how to make the same trip the right way more than once. It facilitates training and coaching by pointing quickly to where a breakdown or deviation is occurring. It underscores that improvement is a process, not a program. And when there are deviations or shortfalls or important next steps that need attention, a diagramed master system gives an efficient way to update senior management with quick, clear compass readings.

Focus Resources

Perhaps the most important value of a well-constructed, clearly diagramed improvement process is that it helps focus resources and effort. The business world wants to improve, and that includes the isolated outposts that can seem sometimes as if they regard headquarters as the enemy or the information source of last resort. That kind of resistance creeps in, especially with independent franchise holders, because it sometimes seems to the geographically dispersed that the parent corporation wants dozens of confusing, unrelated, and sometimes inconsistent efforts.

Steering Around the Detours

The most significant contemporary trend in performance improvement is to develop one clear, consistent, integrated mainstream system. This kind of system earns credibility through consistency. This kind of system is open and dynamic. As better practices and methods emerge, they are scooped into the system to enrich and strengthen it.

Before most businesses adopt a systemic framework, they frequently go through some primitive periods. In a classic instance, one of our major auto companies suddenly saw its costs on repair warranties skyrocket. The auto manufacturer, experienced as it was, turned out to be just as naive and outraged as an inexperienced service purchaser when, having authorized increasingly generous warranty work reimbursement, the bill came due. The warranty cost significantly exceeded expectations—by many millions of dollars.

Big corporations are no different from individual customers. They don't like to be surprised. Unfortunately, sometimes they waste time by getting upset rather than moving forthrightly to get better.

The auto company in question reacted first by calling a series of meetings aimed at encouraging dealers to do a better job of service—lots of cheerleading but little improvement. When the pep talks didn't work, a cynical period set in, so auditors were sent out. But they reported that the dealers were trying their best. The real reason for high warranty cost finally emerged: Dealers at that time just didn't know as much about managing the service side of the business as they knew about the sales side.

Executives of this enlightened manufacturer, after several very human, if time-consuming, detours, decided that they needed a major effort to solve a major problem and created a whole new, long-term framework to improve service. They diagramed an improvement process that took up every phase of the business, set standards, provided real help regarding best practice, and then gave meaningful recognition to those dealers who set out to achieve some sort of supremacy in the service side of their business.

It is taken for granted, sometimes, that commands and orders move people and organizations. It doesn't work that way anymore. People want to know why and how and "what's in it for me," perfectly reasonable questions, given the scope of business change today. And when they're primed to go, they need a good map, a playbook, a diagram—a framework for improvement.

Create a Hinge Point Between Your Business Plan and Your Performance Expectations

Will Rogers used to talk about his "plan" for heating the waters of the Atlantic Ocean. He would elaborate on all the health benefits and the extended swimming season. When asked how he would accomplish this remarkable task, Rogers would say, "I just develop the broad strategies. I leave the details to others."

Ask managers of any progressive business organization about their business plan. They will respond with pride and confidence. Somewhere neatly filed away are the strategies that will lead to a better tomorrow.

Ask those same managers about their track record for accomplishing last year's goals and you frequently get some hesitation. It seems there were a lot of unusual, extenuating circumstances last year.

Then ask for their performance plan. This should be the extension of the business plan that breaks down, with specificity and sensitivity, what the people who are going to make the plan work need to know, do, and feel to achieve the goals.

Developing an action framework is more than pulling out your busi-

ness plan and telling everybody about it. The conversion of business objectives into performance objectives—into matters that human beings
can and will do something about—is a critical and frequently overlooked step. This conversion is the hinge point.

It's surprising how many otherwise sophisticated organizations have
no such human performance plan. Jack Bowsher, former director of
education at IBM and author of *Educating America*, estimates that "95
percent of the Fortune 500 companies would fail an audit on translating
business requirements to performance requirements to education
requirements."[6]

Change in organizations occurs only through people. The business
plan says, here's what the company is trying to get done. The hinge
point of success is connecting the plan to people performance—getting
across to the work force what changes you want; what you want them to
do more of, or less of, or differently; when; why; and what the company
will do to help people reach their potential and meet the demands of
the tasks ahead.

Sophisticated organizations today have people who are skillful in writing business plans. Numbers are scrubbed and challenged with great intensity. Profound themes of improvement are expressed. The plan review process is certainly taken seriously. Approval of the annual plan is
a time of celebration, followed by a period of optimism. But the plan
may well be flawed if nobody has asked:

- Who is going to accomplish all of that?

- Are the human skills, values, and attitudes consistent with the objectives?

- Have the people being counted on to do these wondrous deeds been
  consulted?

- Has proper weight been given to what is standing in the way of accomplishment? Has anybody really looked squarely at why some of
  last year's intentions weren't accomplished?

- Are these plans and objectives meant seriously, or are they just targets?

- What are the rewards for achievement and the consequences for falling short?

- How would the plans be different if the power of people were factored in from the very beginning of the planning process? Has the
  business plan shaped by operating managers, business strategists, and
  financial executives received simultaneous input from those who deal
  with organizational culture, psychology, learning, motivation, communication, and other human resource issues?

Performance Plan Differences

The performance plan flows directly from the business plan, but you should approach this phase of planning with 10 important considerations:

1. Put a priority on people—consider how people do their jobs as a way to achieve additional competitive advantage. This is more than the role of people in implementing other strategies. Human performance is regarded as an important way, in its own right, to achieve product or service differentiation. The process begins with a different question: "What could our people do that they have never done before?"

2. Test business-plan assumptions against the knowledge and skill resources of the organization. Can objectives be accomplished? Is the talent base in place?

3. Structure early involvement of the people who must make the plan work, not only to express what they need but also to recommend better ways.

4. Consider the organizational chart as fluid, not fixed. Be willing to take a fresh look at responsibilities, authorities, reporting relationships, and technological supports in the light of the tasks ahead. This includes innovations in working with other stakeholders—dealers, unions, suppliers.

5. Translate customer needs into business objectives; then translate business objectives into performance requirements.

6. Use a structured process to guide participants through the pain of change; help them move with you from analysis to action to commitment.

7. Capture, treasure, and manage individualized commitments. The commitment process is the key to serious, sustained change in a democratic society.

8. Update standards, curriculum, methods of communication, motivation, recognition, measurement (concepts discussed in subsequent chapters) to be in sync with business initiatives and to help individuals achieve what they have committed to achieve.

9. Support fresh business initiatives with *why* and with examples of best practice so that human beings have a model to follow.

10. Create a dynamic process rather than a static plan. Tie portions of funding to incremental results. Continually raise sights.

This kind of process is a lot different from simply deciding what to teach and what to tell, and makes people-planning integral to strategy formulation. Looking at human performance this way can not only develop stronger people, but can stimulate innovative business initiatives.

After all, sometimes looking at people configurations and performances imaginatively might modify fundamental business priorities and provide new opportunities or different kinds of solutions.

Take, for example, a new high-rise hotel that found itself with patron complaints that the elevators were too slow. The technological solution—to rip out and replace banks of elevators—would have cost a fortune. This hotel's management found a people-centered solution that was a lot simpler and less expensive. The hotel defined the problem as guest satisfaction, impatience, and a perception of slowness. So this hotel was the first to install full-length mirrors between each of the elevators on every floor. Guests would take a few seconds to check their grooming, and that interval was sufficient for them to become satisfied with the timing of the elevators. Since guests received something useful to them, everybody came out a winner. This idea caught on throughout the industry, which explains why there's a common look to many hotel elevator lobbies.

There's a lesson in all this. Business planners at times call for an overabundance of expensive, sophisticated technology, only to find competitors achieving higher output and higher quality by relying more on simpler human systems and solutions.

In thinking boldly about different kinds of people configurations, performances, and systems, it is helpful to consider the experience of the organizational planning consultant who wanted to find out the real difference between heaven and hell. So he arranged for an on-site inspection of both places.

In hell, the consultant found banquet tables groaning with abundant varieties of succulent food. But all the inhabitants had long forks strapped to their arms, so they couldn't get the food to their mouths. That's hell. In heaven, the consultant found identical banquet tables filled with food. These diners also had the long forks attached to their arms. Everything appeared the same. After many questions, the consultant finally figured out the difference. His findings? Upstairs, the diners feed each other, and that imaginative teamwork is what makes it heaven.

This story illustrates the difference between a business force and just a work group. The point is that when you think about people actions with the same imagination that you employ to think about other phases of the business, you increase the chances of the plan's succeeding. And you may alter the plan itself as well as the planning process.

Encourage Flexible Experimentation

Some business plans that stress entrepreneurial thinking and innovation have follow-up mechanisms that are rigid. Instead of unleashing potential, the plan can stultify, put people into well-worn grooves, and overlook big opportunities or competitive threats that arise between annual plan reviews.

If there is incremental profit in a new action, if it will pay for itself and then some, the plan should be open for additions, substitutions, and reprioritizations at any time. Opening up the planning process ought to include the standing invitation for all stakeholders to enrich or modify the plan. This should be more than ad hoc improvising. It should be a regular process to incorporate and give legitimacy to some of the better field adjustments.

Bold alternatives should be encouraged in performance planning by permitting the first discussions of highly imaginative, even outrageous, actions to be circulated for concept reviews, but without the same level of documentation that traditionally accompanies more conventional actions. Sponsors of some of the breakthroughs should be allowed to treat their innovations as real-world experiments. In performance planning, rather than endlessly debating the merits of a new approach, set up a pilot activity. Try a number of alternatives. Human performance development needs its own proving grounds, its own test kitchens. Take advantage of the flexibility of human beings by phasing rather than proclaiming new methods.

Design "Living" Plans

Develop "living" plans, with passion, fire, innovation, and human partnerships built in from the beginning. Plans ought to specify what the company and its people are going to do differently to accomplish forecasted results. Without this emphasis, plans can become an annual recitation of what the company wishes to accomplish, rather than what it is truly armed to achieve.

Provide Examples

Plans meant to be implemented by mortals ought to have sections showing real-world, successful implementation. Too many business planners discard one of the most valuable by-products of the planning process, the evidence upon which the assumptions justifying the need for change are based.

Business plans tend to put the spotlight on bold breakthroughs. Performance plans assume that the bolder the new direction, and the more it differs from current practice, the more a lot of people that you count on are going to have to move through the same discovery processes that planners do to sense for themselves that the new way is better. Human nature and habit must be taken into account. A certain amount of N.I.H., "not-invented-here," must be anticipated. So you collect and value the evidence of where and how new methods are working.

Distribute Performance Plans Imaginatively

Publishing performance plans does not have to be limited to three-ring binders and other conventional packages. In a multimedia era, in an organization that integrates business planning and people planning, the dissemination can have many formats. Business planners can tend to feel that writing the document and doing the economic justifications are the important steps. Performance planners recognize that the key is to get those ideas understood, believed, and acted upon. Computer diskettes, television cassette commentaries, desktop publishing mechanisms that allow local units to easily tailor the plan to local circumstances, are examples of getting the plan out of the desk drawer and into the hearts and minds of the people who are going to make it work.

Conclusion: Raise Sights

A dynamic planning process enables an organization to become comfortable with the notion of raising sights more frequently. The rigidity typical of annual planning is simply not in sync with rapid changes in the marketplace and quick-thrust initiatives by your competitors. While there are inevitably times when new behaviors will take longer than hoped to become ingrained, there also are times when they will be seized more quickly than you expected. Soon the new cutting-edge advantage becomes the new norm. By concept and design, the performance-planning process can be made to push out further without waiting for the next formal planning cycle to begin.

Checklist for Change

☑ Diagram—visualize—the path from where you are to where you want to be so individuals have a shared frame of reference and access to the system.

☑ Spread the idea to build confidence and avoid confusion.

☑ Use the techniques of systems planning.

☑ Allow people to discover for themselves.

☑ Give management and participants a quick snapshot of progress.

☑ Follow the route that's been mapped out. Detour if necessary, but know the reasons why.

☑ Link your business plan to a performance plan.

☑ Test planning assumptions against human capabilities.

☑ Allow the people who must make the plan work to give their input early.

☑ Consider how different people actions or configurations might modify or replace other business actions.

☑ Translate customer needs into business objectives, then into performance requirements.

☑ Encourage flexible experimentation.

☑ Distribute performance plans in imaginative formats that continually adjust and raise sights.

Apply the Learning

Find a business-plan target that has not been met. Analyze the people knowledge, skills, attitudes, and supports that should be in place versus what is in place. Discuss your findings with some of the people who have to do part of their job differently for the plan to be successful. Follow the same analysis-discussion process as it applies to one of your freshest, most important new business goals. Complete the process by defining one fresh initiative, specifying the appropriate people actions with incremental costs and incremental gains.

5

Empower
the Champions
of Change

*It is better to have a thousand lambs led by a
lion, than to have a thousand lions led by a
lamb.*   Anonymous

Who is in charge of the change process is a very important decision. This is
true for the total organization as well as for units within the company. No
matter how fine the grand design for change, rarely will more be accomplished than the leader expects and has the ability to translate to the team.

Finding and empowering champions of change is important for any
organizational initiative, be it a new plant, financial control system, or
marketing plan. But it is especially important in forging partnerships
for performance improvement because the leader will be closely observed and will need to lead by example.

Virtually all businesses have installed the easy improvements, the no-
brainers that everybody agrees are necessary. What lies ahead are improvements of great potential that have not been put in place because there are
intense counterforces. Achieving meaningful change is difficult work. It is
not everybody's desire or highest skill. Managers with a lot of experience and
good administrative capabilities may not necessarily thrive when given major
responsibilities to accomplish serious organizational change.

The Appetite for Change Is Crucial

... A consultant was asking some very pointed questions of the development team. They were working on a powerful human resources system—thoroughly researched, soundly structured, well-funded, and appropriately staffed—but the system wasn't showing the progress or the developmental pace it should have.

The consultant was mystified and reviewed every system characteristic, every decision that had been made. Finally, one of the team members summoned her courage and said,

"I think your inventory is incomplete."

"What do you mean?" the consultant queried.

"Well, you still haven't discussed the appetite for change of the person in charge of the program."

There is an old dictum that says, "Lead, follow, or get out of the way," but there are people in organizations who decline to lead, refuse to follow, and do not move out of the way.

Lackluster leadership is an anomaly in a culture that celebrates personal independence and makes heroes of outstanding performers in music, sports, media, and other art forms. But there's obviously something—or some things—in our corporate system that tends to restrict the quality of leadership and the quantity of leaders.

Four Leadership Situations = Four Opportunities to Improve

Situation 1—Waiting for All the Answers

Six months after one of the Arab oil embargoes had rocked the petroleum industry, the director of marketing for Gulf Oil still had not scheduled meetings with the thousands of worried, confused independent service station owners. He explained the procrastination this way: "We didn't cause the embargo. We still don't understand the implications. We don't know what to tell them." The counsel? "Tell them you don't know. Simply update them on where you are and what you face together."

Leading doesn't mean starting with all the answers. In this age of an educated, inner-directed work force and widely distributed information, too many managers delay mounting an attack on their competitive challenges until they can come to their people with the answers. Granted, it's better to have solutions in hand, but if you don't, clearly laying out the situations you face can convert challenges from threat to thrust. After all, shadows are more fearful than straightforward descriptions of even the most chaotic situation.

Situation 2—Too Many Generals

If I were confronted by a clearly superior army and had only one wish, I would wish that my adversary had seven generals of equal rank. Even if all seven were superb commanders, I submit that a unit with one clear leader could run circles around an army whose seven coequal generals would have to huddle before countering each move.

For example, the leadership of committees is a special art. The first job of a committee is to define its charter and its life span. If these are not clear, the leader needs to provide process steps and tools to hammer out such charters quickly. Committees can assemble a variety of perspectives to reach sound decisions, but if the committee looks at leadership as a collective exercise, progress will be very slow. That same slow pace of continuing negotiation will plague organizations that have their decisions formulated by a number of executives on the same level, without a tiebreaker.

Situation 3—Building on Previously Laid Foundations

Large-scale, long-term systems frequently start with great flourishes and trumpets and achieve notable early success. Some of those who take the place of the originators may feel that if they simply carry on the good work, they will be regarded as caretakers rather than leaders in their own right. As organizations downsize, as the success pyramid becomes narrower and more competitive toward the top, it can be tempting for replacement managers to deprive inherited initiatives of resources and divert efforts to something brand new with a more personal imprint. Evaluations of leadership should recognize those who will build upon the good work that has gone before.

Situation 4—Wasting the Honeymoon

Executives and managers taking on new responsibilities have brief time frames in which to start putting their imprint on events. A period of optimism and good will can be rapidly dissipated by empty rhetoric and trivial, disconnected actions. Potential followers who are eager for new methods, new medicine, and new magic can quickly become restless. Leadership that comes from being anointed is perishable. One keeps leadership by practicing it.

Even with the urgency understood and individual roles grasped, genuine work-force commitment is not ignited without confidence in organizational leadership. Charisma aside, the kind of buy-in discussed in Chapter 2 rests mainly on the worker's instinctive sense that maximum effort is indeed being mobilized and that the mission can succeed. The kinds of turnarounds or large-scale efforts staged by Lee Iacocca at Chrysler, Don Peterson at Ford, Roger Smith at GM, Jack Welch at GE, and elsewhere are good examples.

The bottom line, perhaps, is that business leadership is tough work with a high risk of failure. If you've got it made, as the reasoning goes, why go looking for trouble? Add to that the fact that a tough leader is apt to incur enmity simply because he or she is pressing people to get the job done right. And in big organizations, leaders, by definition, are more single-minded, more aggressive, and therefore more of a nuisance or threat than the more passive players.

Create an Environment for Champions to Step Forward

Empowering leaders has more to do with creating and maintaining an environment in which leadership can emerge than it has to do with the innate characteristics of great leaders. In corporate life today, there are more shackles in the way charters are set up and jobholders positioned than there are shortfalls in the capabilities of individual leaders.

It has always been difficult to find leaders, champions, or deciders willing to step up to a challenge and be counted on for results. Many in leadership roles lack the zest for new tests. Others lack the base and the power to lead.

Tapping the Leadership Surplus

Leadership capability is within far more managers than is generally recognized. Most organizations have substantially more leadership talent than they are using. Concentration should be on liberating that potential by choosing carefully based on appropriate criteria, chartering clearly, and supporting the charter for the long term.

A lot is being written these days about corporate leadership. Some is useful, but much of the popular stuff is hogwash. What gets overlooked is not the qualities of leaders or leadership techniques but the real difficulty of the terrain. Leaders need to be "chartered" or empowered by their organizations to get jobs done—or else to let someone else do them.

Instead of passively assigning roles, senior management is responsible for enabling people to deliver results by specifying and explaining responsibilities in doable and measurable terms. Putting a person "in charge" of sales is one thing. Telling that person, "Your job is to increase sales by 10 percent," is quite another.

Leaders emerge, too, when they become convinced that what they are up to is important and that they have a real opportunity to make a difference. Larger-scale solutions unleash energies by getting people excited. There is vast untapped energy in our work force that lies dormant because people do not feel that their contributions will make a difference. When they are convinced that what is being embarked upon will truly make things better in some significant and long-term ways, the adrenaline starts to flow and they become willing to fold into larger efforts. It is sometimes stunning to see the transformation that comes in personality, style, confidence, and stature when a person is pulled out of a vast bureaucracy and asked to accomplish something that is both clear and clearly important to the organization.

Identifying and Selecting Capable Leaders

Leaders can be classified in any number of ways, both informally and formally. One informal but nonetheless useful scheme ranks leaders into three groups:

1. Those who make things happen
2. Those who let things happen
3. Those who never even know anything is happening

It's the make-things-happen leader who concerns us here. Leadership is taking charge, sharing the vision, setting objectives, establishing a framework, and then leading—simply leading.

Image vs. Substance. Leaders move organizations forward by articulating where they are going and why it will be good to be there. Managers who do not bother to do that may look and talk like leaders, but they really are not. George Jessel used to tell the story of coming home in a captain's uniform and proudly saying to his mother, "Hey, look at me!" And his mother, blunt and cynical, replied, "It's apparent to you that you are a captain, and you are a captain to me. But are you a captain among captains?"

At times, the so-called trappings or superficialities of leadership can be misleading and damaging to end results. Leadership has little, if anything, to do with the tone of command, dressing for success, walking or talking with urgency, or showing intellectual brilliance.

Leadership is not charisma, though the two are often confused. Nor is it, in this new era, boom and bluster and smash. As General (and President) Eisenhower once noted, "You do not lead by hitting people over the head. That's assault, not leadership."

Corporate America is full of titled people who look, talk, and act like leaders but rarely lead on matters of real importance. They manage. They administer. They plan. But they seldom step out front to lead a charge or to champion a cause.

Nailing Down Selection Criteria. Leadership selection is one of the most important decisions in mounting a real attack on an organization's problems. Therefore, leadership designations are not to be made casually. There are several criteria or characteristics that are critical in selecting performance improvement leaders. These criteria are also useful for personal analysis if you are going to put yourself in charge of important changes. Pick a champion who:

- Understands the targeted audience and cares about their problems
- Is willing to listen
- Sees the possibilities of change
- Brings a sense of mission
- Understands the role of knowledge to help people grow
- Understands the role of communication to help people understand
- Is a good communicator, both for clarity of direction and to get people excited
- Is credible and consistent; will earn the right to be listened to
- Has high standards; cares about what happens
- Can give pinpointed counsel to strengthen output
- Will share credit; will build upon other people's foundations, including the work of predecessors
- Is willing to innovate and take measured risks to achieve breakthroughs

- Can build a team, figure out precisely what diverse contributors bring to the end result, and get the best out of them
- Is willing to measure what happens, take the heat and responsibility, and keep the focus on results rather than sideshows
- Will patiently earn receptivity for new ideas, coach, teach, and lead by example and make adjustments when required

Removing Organizational Hindrances to Leadership

If there is a lot more leadership in organizations than is being used, it is especially important for corporations to clear away the environmental hindrances that discourage leaders from emerging. There are a number of organizational, or structural, impediments to getting the job done:

- Organization charts which vaguely define roles rather than the tasks to be accomplished
- Overlapping charters, which leave two or more people vaguely accountable for results, with the predictable result that there is no accountability
- Confusing leadership with the trappings and myths of leadership
- Convoluted decision paths, too many deciders
- Authority not commensurate with responsibility; rewards not commensurate with risks
- Praise for activity rather than results
- Financial procedures that discourage innovation by easily approving expenditures with precedents but fiercely challenge new solutions because "we've done okay without them"
- Innovation without the special nurturing that untried ideas must have

Most organizations do not operate the way their organization charts say they do. Real lines of communication and responsibility often run quite differently from the formal lines. And conventional organization charts compound people problems. The worst feuding can occur among "equals" on the organization chart—the sales VP, the honcho in manufacturing, the marketing director, and others, all of whom have their private agendas. An astonishing amount of energy in big organizations drains away in the feuding, truces, and negotiations formalized in conventional organization charts.

The charts are drawn very passively. They show, for instance, that this person is in charge of sales, that one is in charge of finance, and the other one is in charge of production. Each is dependent on the other, but their goals differ. The financial person is "responsible" for profit improvement, which may hamstring the salesperson trying to boost sales through increased research or marketing.

Senior management often believes—mistakenly—that organization charts give people clear-cut accountability. If great care is not taken, the organization charts can provide places to hide. Top managers can sometimes overlook the fact that upstream decisions have downstream results, as the following anecdote—a true one—well illustrates.

I once saw a tough, decisive manager pull back from a much-needed performance-improvement initiative.

"Did you have good evidence that the organization needed this kind of help?" I asked.

"Yes," he replied.

"Did you have good evidence that the results would far outweigh the costs?" I probed further.

"Yes," he answered again.

"Then why the decision to withdraw from the situation?"

"I backed away," he said, "because the costs will accrue to my operation. The considerable results will show up downstream in the organization, and I don't trust my bosses to understand cause and effect. They will regard me as somebody who exceeded his budget, and they will regard the downstream beneficiary of my operation's efforts as some kind of genius who will be rewarded while I am punished."

That response from an intelligent executive carries with it the essence of why powerful, sustainable organizational improvement is very difficult without the recognition of all of the echelons and factors that must pull together.

Rotating Leadership So That It Is Earned and Reearned

A useful tactic and a good way to explore potential is to rotate leadership responsibilities. Rather than rolling the dice with vast, simultaneous changes in organizational structure and long-term responsibilities, some corporations first test their leaders by giving them the command of sharply focused task groups.

When such task units are freed from day-to-day responsibilities, have clear-cut goals and a set amount of time and funding to make their contribution, a lot of good work can be accomplished rapidly. Sponsoring corporations have a real-life laboratory to observe leadership in action before they cast new functions into organizational stone.

It is surprising that corporations don't make more of an effort to rotate leadership responsibilities. Some organizations do this very skillfully. With leadership roles earned and reearned on the basis of very specific results, if one person can't do the job, you can find another who can—and who will prove it on the testing ground.

A lot of people, not just the leader, must work hard to create and sustain an environment hospitable to the change process. This takes eternal vigilance and clear-eyed analysis, because bold new directions are proclaimed with flourish and fanfare, but the hindrances accumulate slowly and quietly. A new procedure, a memo, a mindless rebuke, the careless expression of a contradictory priority: All creep into day-to-day organizational life, and champions shrug and quietly withdraw to the safety of the crowd and solaces outside of work.

Conclusion: Toward an Empowered Leadership

Empowerment is not simply giving somebody a title. The bolder the ideas and the stronger the champion, the more important it is to give that person the kind of environment that nurtures, rewards, and makes the resources of the organization readily available. This monitoring of the environment needs to be an ongoing process.

Let's face it, real leadership entails some career risks. Some cautious executives have found that it is possible to fill the days administering and planning while letting others take the heat and absorb the injuries from bold initiatives.

Organizations are complex places today. It is not always clear where contributions are coming from. It is possible to sound like a leader without ever taking the actions, and the risks, that should be part of the leadership mantle.

Management of human resources is an art form, and nurturing leadership in big organizations is difficult. Yet when management tries to figure out where an organization's strength really is, it invariably comes down to people and their ability to lead.

We are now completing Part 1 on the front end of big, serious, and sustained productivity improvement, and we haven't yet discussed staging a meeting, writing a script, producing a video report, purchasing new technology, proclaiming a dramatic new theme, or many of the other tangible actions that are associated with the development of people.

Instead, the emphasis has been on the *foundations* for long-term, continuous productivity improvement—foundations that too many restless people hurry past, dooming themselves and their organizations to circular and repetitive activities. We've looked at actions that are key at the beginning stages of forging productivity partnerships:

1. Start with what is important to the customer.
2. Round out a fully dimensioned situational assessment.
3. See reality through the eyes of the people you are counting on.
4. Recognize that sharing the challenge can get people stirred.
5. Portray a clear vision that others see and understand.
6. Sharpen your interpretive skills and enlarge the scope of your thinking and the scale of your efforts to match the size and persistence of the problems you are facing.
7. Diagram a framework so that the process of moving from current reality to a better way is clear and open to all participants.
8. Support your business plan with a synchronized performance plan.
9. Guide people through an analysis-commitment-action process.
10. Manage the individual commitments.
11. Ignite these elements of change with the explosive spark of empowered leadership.

With these important foundations in place, you see your forward directions clearly. Now you are ready to consider the wide range of tools and techniques to move your business strategies, and their knowledge, skill, and attitude components, into the hearts and minds of the people who must make the strategies work.

Checklist for Change

☑ Keep leadership an open society, an attainable goal.

☑ Identify people who get things done.

☑ Recognize replacement managers for building on the sound work of predecessors.

☑ Choose leaders carefully, a key decision.

☑ Forget the trappings of leadership; use selection criteria relevant to the tasks.

☑ Clear away the hindrances to leadership.

☑ Give charters in terms of results.

☑ Avoid overlapping charters.

☑ Make resources and supports readily available.

☑ Have leadership earned, reearned, and rotated.

Apply the Learning

Find an initiative, big or small, and lead.

PART 2

Build Organizational Success Around Individual Success

You have a clear view of what you want to accomplish. You depend upon other people to achieve ambitious goals. You have an increasingly varied array of tools and techniques available. Now we consider how you put the methods together so that they reinforce each other, so that some thrust develops, so that the organization starts to *move forward*.

The key is to provide assistance on an individualized, prescriptive basis. That means *integrating* strategy, operations, knowledge, skill, information, marketing support, technology, organizational communication, and motivation.

Part 2 analyzes the potentials at your command to teach and reach, looking at training, communication, and motivation techniques not as separate disciplines, but as elements that can be *coalesced* for significant and consistent change.

The same principles that can help turn a work force into a powerful business force can also be applied immediately to your reports, presentations, and day-to-day managerial communicating and coaching.

6

Aim for Audiences of One with Prescriptive Intent

Ideas have to be wedded to action. If there is no vitality to them, there is no action. Ideas cannot exist alone in the vacuum of the mind. Ideas are related to living.
                                        HENRY MILLER

Start by Clarifying What You Mean by Audience and Purpose

In moving from the planning into the action phase of forging partnerships for productivity, managers might find themselves comforted or stimulated by seeing groups of employees gathered in front of them to hear the full story of the new directions they plan to undertake.

But the words "group" and "full story" are carry-overs of an already bygone era of communicating with and developing the work force.

There may be times when *all* of the people and *all* of the information are appropriate, but those instances should be increasingly rare in the 1990s and beyond. You get results from individuals—one person at a time, one improvement at a time. Those individuals have varying backgrounds, experiences, needs, and business assignments. Therefore the productive, contemporary way to start the action phase of performance improvement is by laying out two clear definitions:

1. *Precisely define your target audience.* Develop a clear focus on who, exactly, you're trying to reach, what their problems are, and what they need from you, from each other, and from other stakeholders to be more successful.
2. *Define your purposes* for bringing people together, with particular emphasis on follow-up action.

In today's pressurized, information-rich environment, there are inappropriate ways to communicate the whys and wherefores of performance improvement:

- Casually—as it occurs to you
- Routinely—because you always bring that group together at this time
- Wastefully—by bringing trainees farther than they should travel; by telling them things they already know or things peripheral to their immediate challenges and success

This chapter concentrates on intentional, prescriptive techniques of assembling and training a business force for accomplishments that are beyond their current experience.

Keep the Focus on Results

Adults want results, answers, benefits. Classes, meetings, workshops, seminars, and other organizational communications events are not ends in themselves. They are means to an end. Training is to performance improvement what dieting is to weight reduction. Nobody particularly likes to diet, at least no one I know of, but they do like to look attractive. A prescriptive approach to employee education lets you offer assistance in concert with how adults think and act.

Techniques for Gaining
Audience Receptivity

Target One Person

Marketing 101 teaches marketers to "segment." Who would question that retirees and teenagers, even when buying the same products, should usually be addressed with different appeals and vocabularies? Yet even corporations that are advanced in their marketing still gather employees and franchise holders in big groups for overgeneralized, lockstep messages.

You will sharpen your focus regarding who to address and what to communicate when you think in terms of audiences of one. There is a reason why speech coaches counsel presenters, whether at the lectern or in front of a TV camera, to establish eye contact and chat conversationally. That's the way experienced speakers earn the reaction, "It was as if he was talking directly to *me*." The notion of individualization has implications far beyond the tone and words of a presentation. At the very least, break audiences down into more manageable groups. Get as close as is possible to talking to individuals as individuals.

Thinking in terms of individuals forces you to think of different ways to try to convey messages.

Assemble Audiences for Action

Start with Those Who Will Innovate and Show the Way. When introducing major new initiatives in an organization, it is far more effective to start with small contingents of the willing, those who really need what is being communicated or who are most receptive to the kind of pioneering being advocated. Let a small group start the movement and record some successes. Then go after ever-wider segments a little later, not only with the original concepts but with those concepts now fleshed out by the experiences of the pioneers. Carefully chosen "forerunner" groups have more at stake, are more highly motivated, and will give you livelier participation and faster payback.

Assemble Groups Imaginatively. Assembling groups in imaginative ways, related to the business results desired, is one of the first dividends of the planning issues dealt with in Part 1. When you have a strategy for

productivity enhancement, meetings, courses, and other communications conduits are put into perspective as means to an end, not as ends
in themselves. Everything from invitation lists to agendas come to be
formulated in different ways. Among other ways that audiences can be
gathered, consider:

- *By locality or region.* In view of the technology available today, it
  can be much more cost-effective to take the message to the learner,
  saving travel costs and time away from the job. Using techniques of
  self-pacing, you can get *very* close to the work site. This not only saves
  money, but you can tailor facts, figures, and examples more closely to
  the day-to-day experiences of a specific local audience.

- *By commonality of challenge.* Using business records or pretests, it
  is possible to pinpoint those in greatest need of this or that kind of
  help. When people share common problems, they can be an important resource to each other.

  For example, one innovative national chain arranged bus tours in
  which an area's independent franchise holders visited each other's
  places of business. Each owner discussed areas of particular strength
  or need. Headquarters received an extra dividend in that the franchisees, in getting ready to host their peers, installed a flurry of improvements to use as examples of the kind of progress they were making.

- *By similarity of situation.* For example, all of the biggest or most
  sophisticated distributors or dealers can be dealt with together in one
  gathering, the smaller dealers in another. That way, material is scaled
  to their respective needs and work team members bring more com-
  patible perspectives.

- *By a diagonal slice of different perspectives and responsibilities.* Bringing together disparate, even sometimes uncooperative
  forces—bosses and subordinates, management and union, or other
  people who normally don't work together—can produce a stimulating
  mix. For example, if you have field representatives who contact franchise dealers, mixing the two groups and getting them to articulate
  what they expect from each other may yield surprising breakthroughs.

- *By linking other important stakeholders and influencers.* Organizational communications efforts, even long-term ones, influence people for just a small part of their lives. Each individual has his or her
  own real-life orbit. That can be made to work for you. For selected
  initiatives, especially bold ones that involve new directions or the potential of big rewards, managers might want to include spouses, children, or other family members. It is conceivable even to create some

events exclusively for these significant others whose support is so important.

Inventory What Has Preceded the Event

Coping with the "Noahs" in Your Organization.   Perhaps you've heard or read the story of the survivor of a great raging flood who spent the rest of his life telling all who would listen, and many who wouldn't, about those angry, swirling waters. When he died, he went to heaven and found to his delight that an audience of millions could be gathered to hear his story. There was unlimited time. Ecstatic with the opportunity, the new arrival asked if there were any constraints.

St. Peter answered, saying, "This vast gathering has eternity to listen. But just remember, as you tell about your experiences, somewhere out there in that audience is Noah."

Here on earth, out there among the people you are trying to move to excellence, there are a *lot* of Noahs—adults who bring lifetimes of rich and varied experiences to their jobs and their relations with other employees, supervisors, subordinates, suppliers, and customers. That's something that should be respected and built upon.

So before you invite one of these Noahs to your next meeting, training program, or whatever, ask yourself some questions:

"What do I want him or her to know, do, and feel afterward that is not in place now?"

"What kind of gathering is this?"

Decision?	Motivation?
Learning?	Celebration?
Practice and reinforcement?	Review of work progress?
Information? (Is there an easier way to convey it?)	Fresh assignment or commitment?

Combinations are okay as long as they are deliberate, and not a sign of muddled purpose.

Don't Stop with Mere Data; Get a Sense of Those Experiences.   Politeness in business can mask negative emotions. Frustration is the common cold of the business world. You might be surprised at the accumulation of small resentments that can lie beneath an otherwise placid exterior. Those attitudes can range from stark fear to seething rage.

Inventorying what has preceded you is more than just collecting previously delivered information. You want a sense of those earlier experiences, good or bad, that have colored receptivity. Adults bring a history with them. In that history can be:

- Corporate promises unkept
- Battles begun with great flourish and then ended without telling the "warriors," who kept on fighting
- Superiors who reported results in ways that those closest to the action felt were distorted or unfair
- Communications that showed little respect for the intelligence or integrity of the intended recipients

Responsibility for Employee Time Starts at the Top. If you want the work force to do something new and important, be prepared to earn your way into the mind, past the gates of battle-scarred cynicism. If you don't want them to do something new and important, don't bring them together. There are other, easier ways to convey information today.

If you, as manager, boss, or supervisor, want more yield per time spent on the job, then you must not exempt yourself from a disciplined process. You are responsible for saving employee time by getting to the point and sticking to published agendas. The "fast forward" feature that is part of today's omnipresent videocassette recorders provides a kind of viewer control that needs to be carried over to the world of an organization's internal communications. When you save your employees' or colleagues' time, you not only save money, you send a signal of urgency, efficiency, and respect that becomes part of the learning experience.

I once was in attendance at a presentation in which the branch manager of a nationally known organization, surprised by a visitor representing the home office, felt obliged to apologize for the number of chart pages clipped together for omission from the material headquarters had provided. Yet it was this field exec who was owed the apology. If those pages could so easily be skipped, then they shouldn't have been included in that area's version of the national presentation in the first place.

Whenever you're contemplating the cost of communications and training, don't fail to take into account the value of the time of the people who will be consuming the message. Valuing time means providing help and support in excess of the value of the time you are asking your audience to invest.

Prescriptiveness in Training Means Relevance

The Teachable Moment

... You are at a party and a stranger corners you and starts to tell you in great detail about the 10 best restaurants in Copenhagen. He describes the menus and the decor of each establishment with enthusiasm and excruciating exactitude. You quickly look around for a way to escape this stranger, whom you've sized up as either a colossal bore or a certifiable nut.

Wouldn't it be a far different story if this stranger told you that he was acquainted with some of the best restaurants in Copenhagen, presented one brief example to whet your appetite, and invited you to call him if you were ever traveling to Denmark?

As fate would have it, some time later your company is sending you to Copenhagen for a week. Now you would happily contact this individual and listen attentively, perhaps even make some notes, as he recounted his culinary experiences. You are at "the teachable moment," the time when you want and need the information because you are going to do something with it.

Prescriptive learning taps into three important current trends:

1. Business is complex, turbulent, and changing. There is a glut of information, and there are increasing amounts to communicate and teach to the work force.

2. Adults learn best and quickest to solve specific problems.

3. Today's information technologies permit concepts to be retrieved on demand: in effect, "just-in-time" learning.

Making training prescriptive means:

- Giving learners what they need.
- Giving it when it's needed.
- Giving help that is industry-specific, task-specific, learner-specific, and success-specific.
- Allowing the trainee to move rapidly past what is already known through life experience to what is novel and useful.
- Interacting with the knowledge and skill support at a pace that is com-

fortable for the learner. Mastery of the material is virtually assured
for the learner who will commit the effort. The variable shifts from
"whether" that person learns to "how long it takes."

Relevance in business means communication anchored to what is important to the organization and to the individuals on the receiving end,
whether they be customers, suppliers, or the work force. It is the reason
that all managers, not just training and communication specialists, must
insert themselves forcefully into the education and communication activities of their organization. Finished work gets its power not simply
from polished prose or powerful images but from the clear-cut inter-
connection between what is being taught and communicated and how
the organization is going to measure and reward its people.

Avoid Junk Food for the Mind

Information is doubling every 5 years. In *Information Anxiety*, author
Richard Wurman points out that a weekday edition of *The New York
Times* contains more information than the average person was likely to
come across in a lifetime in seventeenth-century England.[7]

In other research, Dr. Ralph Nichols pioneered a course at the University of Minnesota on effective listening. He documents that students
listen about 50 percent of the time, tuning in and out at intervals.

In a learning situation, we retain:

- 25 percent of what we hear
- 45 percent of what we hear and see
- 70 percent of what we hear, see, and do[8]

These percentages assume that the information we are exposed to is
useful and relevant. In fact, most of what crosses our desks or that surrounds us in public media is not that relevant. Even useful information
often comes buried under layers of data we already know or don't care
about. We criticize junk food as being bad for our physical health. We
must realize that there is also junk food for the mind. Platitudes, piecemeal bits of information, redundancies, and irrelevancies can clog
thinking and provide no practical sustenance.

Forced throughout most of our waking hours to defend ourselves
from information overload, our filtering mechanisms shut down. We
don't necessarily know what to take in and what to exclude. There is no
better way for any manager to establish a real partnership with people
than to develop a reputation for "input responsibility"—the assurance

that what is being asked, taught, communicated, or measured is main-stream to the business and tightly connected to how the individual succeeds.

Convert Data into Action

Data becomes valuable only when it is used as a basis for action. There is a process which, if followed, yields a reliable means for transforming raw data into value-added action:

- Skim off the data that has potential meaning to the particular user.
- Convert the data into information—data that has meaning to the particular user.
- Convert the information into learning—information that becomes part of thinking patterns.
- Convert learning into action—knowledge and skill that are applied to achieve results.

Gear to How Adults Like to Learn

Adults prefer to learn differently from children. Therefore, how assistance is developed for them should be built on certain principles and should put you in a position to state clear-cut benefits.

- Design training around important problems. "What you invest time in is connected to your real world."
- Make training immediately applicable. "Take the knowledge and skills back to your job and use them."
- Build on previous experience. "You get credit for what you already know."
- Provide learner control. "You can move rapidly past what you already feel comfortable with and spend more time on what is new and important to you."
- Invite active participation. "Don't just sit there. Think proactively about what this means to you. Experiment with applications."
- Sequence material to move from whole to part to whole. "See how it all fits together. Then examine the elements. Then put the elements back together so that you can use them."

- Encourage integrative, holistic thinking. "Learn to learn and to integrate new mastery with how you conduct your business."

- Accommodate individual learning rates and styles. "You have your own way of learning. We will serve the material that way."

- Provide checks for understanding and feedback. "We will listen and test to make sure you comprehend and to keep improving what we offer."

Design for Participation. Involvement means creating a sense of participation or partnership with those at whom the "change" message is directed. What do they need? Listen and they will tell you. Ironically, many organizations that pride themselves on a commitment to communication fear spontaneous, two-way communication. They so sanitize and control their messages that the life juices are removed. At times, you need the clash of ideas for recommended methods to demonstrate their legitimacy.

The kind of active participation needed from people can be made or broken by the way meetings and courses are designed. Questions and answers, role-play, practice, simulation, and small discussion groups guide learners away from standard passive mode. You want their experiences, challenges, fears, and ideas to work for you. It is an essential factor in adult-level learning for trainees to take an active hand in their own development. In this way, not only program materials but also fellow attendees become valuable resources to draw upon. Even the best plans are theoretical until you add people to the mix. Each group takes on a life of its own. A particular group facing a particular set of challenges represents a one-of-a-kind, perishable situation. That particular chemistry didn't exist earlier and will never exist quite that way again.

Speak Their Language. First-class international meeting facilities have United Nations-type translation booths and headsets for each member of the audience. Nobody would be foolish enough to address a German audience in Spanish or a Korean audience in Japanese. Yet organizations routinely convene people and talk to them in stilted, theoretical "headquarterese." Use the language and the experiences of those on the receiving end.

I've watched senior corporate executives address such concrete, localized problems as reducing plant absenteeism from the lofty perspective of international economic trends. By contrast, the union representative at the same function told fellow workers plainly that if absenteeism stayed at current levels, the people who normally clean the bathrooms would be drafted as replacements and the johns would be filthy. One of the consequences of absenteeism was thus described in a way that was clear and personal to every audience member.

At a sales meeting for independent franchise holders, executives presenting sophisticated analysis of trends and needs felt that they had made an important sale. Yet, when a tough, practical entrepreneur was asked what he got out of the analysis, he honed in quickly on the issue: "The manufacturer has some hot products that are in short supply, and I won't get enough of them. The manufacturer also has some less successful products that it wants me to take more of, and I am not going to do it." Business audiences collectively cut to the heart of the message very quickly. Managers gain by doing things with the audience's benefit in mind and serving up challenges in terms of audience self-interest.

Tailor Material for Immediate Follow-Up Application. You can get more mileage out of time spent and dollars paid out by getting trainees' minds in gear early. Supplying them with a workbook outline well in advance of any given meeting or course is a common way to do this. Such workbooks provide a structured way to gather experiences and questions—the trainees' own as well as those of colleagues and customers.

Give participants material to convey to the people with whom they interface—bosses, associates, customers—what they are learning so that the environment they return to is supportive.

At the training function itself, participants can take notes in the workbooks in a way that is formatted in advance to yield a personalized follow-up action plan. The more that meetings, seminars, and other events can be tailored to the way the participants will actually use the material afterward, the better the chances that the information and learning will be fruitfully applied. If material is organized the way customers ask about the product or service, for example, or if information is sequenced step-by-step the way a task is performed, those on the receiving end understandably feel more comfortable with it.

Concentrate on Content. Content is the very heart of business communication. What do you know that the people listening to you do not know? Much of business is repetitive; everything cannot be new. Nevertheless, reinforcing challenges and assertions with fresh, illustrative specifics moves you away from stagnation. Otherwise, business communication can become a litany, similar to religious services in an archaic language. It is comforting in its familiarity, but most of those saying the words as well as those listening to them have lost sight of what they really mean.

Those illustrative specifics are examples of real-world practices that document and flesh out key points and provide new information and insights. Up-to-the-minute information is your material for building strong, useful assistance.

Speed over Aesthetics

Timing is a matter of getting the material out when the targeted users want and need it. In fast-breaking situations, too many people spend too much time playing with the clay. Information is most valuable when it is still warm. With abundant technologies of simultaneous transmission to remote field locations, the slow point in the process can be prettying up the message. For new information, speed takes precedence over aesthetics. The perishability of information is an important reason to strategize communication in waves. In that way, information can be moved quickly and then codified in longer-term-use formats as part of the next wave of effort.

Plan for Silence

Just as pauses in the delivery of a speech give texture to the presentation, so planned interludes of silence should be part of effective long-run communication and learning strategy.

Silence is to organizational communication what white space is to advertising. It frames and underscores the key message. Silence is preferable to organizational communication that trivializes, simply repeats things said previously, or, worst of all, contradicts and confuses. Silence does not refer to the social interaction or routine reporting that is an everyday part of business. But when you are communicating to achieve long-range results, planned silence is an important element. You need to strategize planned silences so that when you talk, people will listen.

Conclusion: Toward New Paradigms, Patterns, and Methods

When you are crystal clear on audience and purpose, dozens of different decisions that tend to be looked at separately, from location to theme to content, start to be made in more coherent, reinforcing, and result-producing ways.

Sharpened focus on audience and purpose will propel you away from yesterday's habits and toward today's faster, more practical, more effective ways for people to receive information, learn, and rapidly put to work what they have learned.

Prescriptive learning is the way of the future. Corporations will come into that future at various rates of speed. The constraint will not be the needs of the organization, the receptivity of the learner, or the capabilities of the technologies. The limiting factor will be the ability of managers to clearly define where the business is going and what they want people to know and do better to actualize that vision.

Checklist for Change

☑ Target the individual. Think in terms of audiences of one.

☑ Precisely define your audience—who they are, what their problems are, what they need.

☑ Define your purposes for bringing people together—information, decision, learning, practice and reinforcement, motivation, review, fresh assignment. Keep a focus on what you want to happen afterward.

☑ Assemble groups for action. Consider who will spearhead innovation, how to get the learning closer to the learner, how to bring together stakeholders who can be resources to each other.

☑ Inventory what has preceded current activities. Value the time of attendees. Value continuity.

☑ Seize the teachable moment. Let individuals retrieve what is relevant to success, when it is relevant.

☑ Cut through the clutter. Distill information to its essence. Convert data into action. Save learner time.

☑ Train the way adults like to learn.

☑ Stimulate preparation and participation.

☑ Concentrate on content, what you know that your audience does not.

☑ Use the language of the people you bring together. Listen. Get energy from the audience.

☑ Stimulate application—organize material the way the users will actually use it.

Apply the Learning

For your next major communication or training endeavor—be it meeting, course, or whatever, develop an audience and purpose profile. Be specific about the follow-up actions that you expect. Then when all is done, analyze whether you accomplished the purpose.

Next time you are in a long meeting or have to travel a distance to a learning event, analyze how much of the material might better have been formatted prescriptively, for *your* retrieval when you face the situation being taught.

7
Set Standards
That Show
What You Expect

The secret of management is to never make a decision which ordinary human beings cannot carry out.   PETER DRUCKER

Follow a Disciplined Process

Some organizations set performance standards; others do not. Some managers insist standards be followed; others insist on nothing. Some companies press toward higher standards; others just dawdle along.

As a manager, being clear and consistent about what you want increases your chances of achieving it. When what you want is connected to what your customers value and is delivered consistently, then your organization will earn points in the marketplace.

The way to achieve clarity and consistency of goals is to set standards:

In writing

Collaboratively with the holders of each position in your operation

Illustrated by examples of superior practice

Measurable by objective evaluators

Supported by resources that help people achieve the standards

Partnerships built on these foundations will endure. But it means squeezing the vagueness out of organizational understandings. Setting standards has to be a disciplined process. Times of large-scale, rapid change, like now, are good for standing back and taking a new look.

Standards are the requirements for a complete organizational function, the jobs within that function, and the major duties, outputs, and tasks of each position.

Evaluators are measurements that help bosses and the holder of any given position to agree that the standards are being met or to take corrective action. Wherever possible, it is best for evaluators to be objective, not subjective. In that way, there is less potential for disagreement over whether tasks are being performed to standard.

Standards and evaluators should be developed according to a uniform process. Figure 7-1 outlines such a process.

In a standards-based system, standards and evaluators are central to all important people actions, from original hiring (against standards), to teaching and coaching (against standards), all the way to recognition for meeting or exceeding targeted levels of accomplishment.

Setting standards encourages everyone with a stake in the outcome—bosses, subordinates, and peers—to focus on the process involved in doing the work. With business methods changing, customers subtly altering their buying habits, and competitors jockeying for new position, the time is right for many organizations to take a new look at how their business is being conducted.

Standards = Leverage for Excellence

Top-notch companies build the value of standards into everything, from manufacturing processes to hiring and training. Standards put those in charge of policy creation and implementation in a position to say:

- Here is what it is agreed you will do.
- Let us show you how to do it and help you to be successful.
- Let us emphasize how important it is for you to do it this way *consistently*. The level of performance you are being asked for has become something customers expect—a reason to do business with us, our reason to uphold rigorous standards.
- Look around and you will find your behavior reinforced by coworkers who also—consistently—do it the same way. Because there is con-

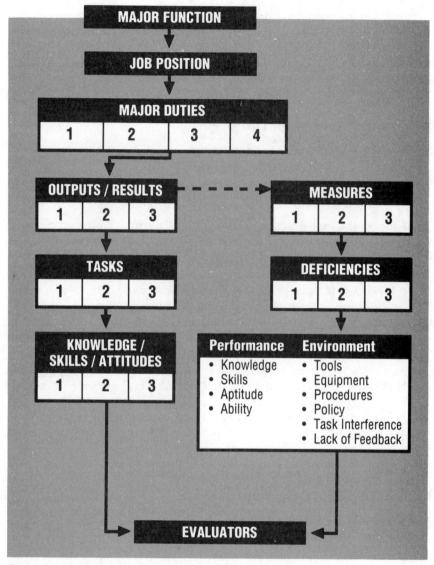

Figure 7-1. Process steps to develop standards and evaluators.

sistency in implementation, our customers, colleagues, and suppliers are able to count on established levels of response.

- When it is time for you to be appraised, promoted, or considered for a raise or other recognition, you will find the criteria used for those decisions revolves around these same standards of performance.

Ideally, there would be precise definitions and exact measurements for every business task, just as there are in most manufacturing processes. Setting standards for the way work is to be performed is easier, in any case, than setting standards for each individual worker.

Where to Go for Input to a Code of Standards

1. Ask your customers what matters most.

2. Find the various in-house performers who are best at every phase of the job and develop a composite superstar model.

3. Draw on the best practices outside. This can draw from competitors in your industry or practices you respect in other industries.

4. Research the field to determine good, better, and best.

To forge a true partnership for productivity, standards should be set in collaboration with a sampling of those holding each job. You get good information, and later the standards will be better received as a tool for self-analysis. It is important to forge standards in a partnership mode, that is, not as judgment from "on high" but as an aid to your employees as associates. Organizations without standards-based systems really do have standards. It's just that nobody has bothered to codify, clarify, or explain them. It will help morale and teamwork if you are clear and consistent about what you expect.

Seven Benefits of a Standards-Based System

Standards as a Basis for Making Jobs More "Playable"

There was once a baseball manager who got fed up with the performance of his shortstop. In a crucial game, the manager inserted himself at short and promptly made several errors. Returning to the dugout in an embarrassed rage, he wheeled on the young shortstop, yelling at him, "You got the position so screwed up, nobody can play it."

Peter Drucker calls certain jobs "widow makers," named after ships that were so perpetually unlucky that their crews felt their lives were in peril. When it became virtually impossible to find sailors willing to set out on such star-crossed vessels, owners frequently made the decision to destroy the ships, even though they might be structurally sound. Today, likewise, certain jobs can't be sailed and are doomed to repetitive failure because the characteristics called for are contradictory traits in combinations that are not easily found. Those jobs need to be pinpointed and either changed to fit the times and available talent pools or eliminated.

Management author and lecturer George Odiorne reports a consistent 25 percent variation between how bosses and subordinates look at job expectations. The process of setting standards allows a manager to focus on what is important and get rid of the clutter of the unimportant, thus making jobs more playable.

Standards as a Basis for Teamwork

No position or individual stands alone in an organization. Therefore, if standards are laid out for a number of positions simultaneously, it becomes easier to understand how the tasks involved fit together. It's like putting together the pieces of a puzzle. It is not uncommon for leaders to preach teamwork but neglect to set up the tasks to fit smoothly into one another to produce the most effective work flow.

But in well-run companies, standards for hiring, training, coaching, evaluating, rewarding, and promoting are all in alignment. That's aimed at getting the right people for the right job for both the short term and the long run.

The advantages are clear. With people costs averaging 70 percent of the typical American company's expenses, anything that reduces turnover and increases performance has a high payout.

Standards as a Basis for Self-Management

In a simpler world, supervisors could easily observe the pace and output of the work force. As thinking becomes a larger part of job content and as operations become more geographically dispersed, standards provide a more contemporary, practical way to manage. Managers and staff become partners dedicated to helping each individual to reach full potential. Teaching individuals to manage themselves against standards requires extra effort. But once a self-directed, standards-based process is in place, every individual is far more aware of his or her own day-to-day performance levels than any external surveillance could possibly accomplish.

The more individuals take responsibility for meeting clear-cut standards, the fewer inspectors you need.

Standards as a Basis for Motivation

Setting standards position by position is rewarding in its own right. The value increases when you design your business's training curriculum, career path development, technological supports, and reward systems around an up-to-date, well-communicated description of what you expect from each position. You get maximum value from a standards-based system when you build motivation, reinforcement, and support around the system.

Retailers know that one of the most common complaints about sales people is that customers are not waited on promptly. In situations in which commission sales people wait for their next "ups," it is possible to calculate a reasonable amount of time an entering customer should remain unattended. You simply figure out how long it takes to come in the front door and move to inspect the merchandise. One well-known retailer solved this customer service problem by painting the floor in several colors. Whereas a customer might think that this is purely decorative, it is used to emphasize the importance of quickly greeting the customer. If a new prospect moves out of the first color zone and hasn't yet been greeted, that visitor no longer belongs to the salesperson whose turn to greet was next but to whoever is most alert and motivated to get to the customer. This is a clear case in which promptly greeting the customer receives practical reinforcement in the form of greater commissions.

Standards as a Basis for Recognition

Honor Achievement Formally, and Make the Honor Meaningful.   Accomplishment in standards-based systems needs to be certified. Reaching a higher level of performance should be honored in formal ways and made operationally significant. When, for example, an insurance agent can put CLU (Chartered Life Underwriter) on a calling card, that credential has impact. The customer feels more confident that the advice is sound. For the designation to continue to have meaning, the trust must be earned. There must be a close correlation between the designation of excellence and the quality of real-world performance. That kind of recognition is best assured if a standards-based system is in place.

Create a Ladder of Accomplishment.   Consistent excellence in every phase of doing business is not easily attained. Excellence is too often viewed as a faraway destination, an aspiration rather than everyday achievement. Recognition can crystallize levels of performance—good, better, and best—and honor specific attainments which, over time, build into significant achievement.

In karate, for example, different colored belts are awarded to mark levels of mastery. Such a system serves simultaneously as recognition and as a motivational system.

Standards as a Basis for Raising the Bar

Improvement in business should *not* be looked at as a program but as a process which has the potential of getting better and better. A significant part of any competitive activity—business, sports, or any other—is mental.

In the anxiety-ridden business environment most corporations face today, it is only human for some people to retreat to the more comfortable, less demanding elements of their jobs. They can devote inordinate time to tasks that people of less skill and less expense could easily do, or tasks for which technology could make a productive contribution.

A process of meeting standards helps the organization to understand that what constituted excellence yesterday should periodically be notched up. Certification gives you good information to decide when raising the bar might be in order, and to create receptivity for the process of continuously getting better.

A good sports analogy is track. In track, the 4-minute mile stood as an unbreakable barrier for 86 years. Once it was broken, however, three other performances of under 4 minutes were turned in within the next 48 months.

When analyzing performance in light of standards, you look at jobs from a new perspective. It is thus possible to see if work can be performed in ways that improve how you are perceived in the marketplace. Done collaboratively, this can defuse frictions that tend to build up over time. When standards are tied to a long-term improvement system and people know they will get help, there is increased receptivity to "upskilling" the job, and less concern about being replaced by a machine.

Standards as a Basis for Consistent Quality

A standards-based certification system is equally valuable in getting consistency into the efforts of independent franchise networks and other arrangements in which local operations are loosely or firmly bound by policies made elsewhere. This is especially true when people are a big part of the customer satisfaction equation. Franchise relationships have grown increasingly prickly lately. The product or service provider owns the marque and is responsible for creating product advantages that will keep it a symbol of excellence, but local entrepreneurs have substantial funds and egos invested in their enterprises too.

The value of any franchise depends upon the consumers' expectations of consistent treatment whenever they see the advertised trademark or symbol. When franchises in an industry are first established, business leaders and advertising copywriters and artists give the trademark its original meaning. But after a period, real-world experiences in the marketplace create the value of the marque.

In a mobile society, with 17 percent of the population living in a different home today than a year ago, the real value of a franchise is the regionwide or nationwide promise the sign holds out for superior treatment. But superior treatment will not happen with consistency unless it is taught, enforced, and recognized. This is something the franchise owner owes not just to headquarters but to all the women and men who have invested in other territories of the same franchise.

The trend in franchising is to specify expected human performance standards in enough detail to serve as a shared frame of reference, enforceable as a contractual franchise obligation. This is the business equivalent of a prenuptial agreement. It is the way the freshness of the hamburger, the crispness of the french fries, the cleanliness of the hotel room, and the expertise of the sales and service functions are quality-assured.

Differentiate Between Principle and Practice

Whether dealing with an independent franchise point, an employee, a supplier, or any other stakeholder, it is not the concern of headquarters to be the last word on every detail of doing business. A dynamic, standards-based system encourages judgment.

In setting standards, then, it is useful to separate principles from practices. *Principles* are the main elements of the position, the way you want the position played. The principles are constant, for example: "To satisfy the customer, each prospect will be greeted within 30 seconds." You take a stand on the ways that you want business done.

At the same time, you can give a lot of latitude in actual practices, the infinite variations in the way a task can be accomplished. If the standard stipulates that the customer will always be offered a product demonstration, this can be done by way of trial use of the product, by discussing the product in the showroom with supporting visuals, or by using props to dramatize one or several product attributes that convey a sufficient impression of superiority. You can give a lot of leeway on practice. As you give this latitude and maintain continual monitoring of real-world performance, you can start to collect and disseminate the most imaginative variations to all the other practitioners. In this way, standards are supplemented by a continually enriched mix of applied ideas.

Conclusion: The Cornerstone of Success

The common characteristic of all successful companies is this: At some point, its managers have thought through every phase of their business, and they run it according to the standards they set. So customer treatment at a Disney theme park, for example, does not depend upon how attendants Susie or Joe feel that morning. The hospitality and the warmth are looked at as part of what customers are buying when they purchase a ticket.

Standards, then, serve as a yardstick against which to measure performance. They define what's acceptable, what's unacceptable, what's good, what's better, what's best. Standards help everybody involved to agree on what constitutes success—and where improvement is required.

When standards are set right, the ultimate test is this: Are you getting the results desired? If the answer is yes, there's obviously no problem. But when people performing against standards fall short, a pattern of need emerges which should be addressed with training or other assistance. Ignoring the standards or lowering them is bad business.

Checklist for Change

☑ Analyze each phase of your business and each performance that contributes to success.

☑ Define requirements for a total function and each position within the function. Be clear on major duties, tasks, and outputs.

☑ Develop evaluators that objectively help both you and the holders of jobs to measure performance against standards and to correct deficiencies.

☑ Describe what constitutes superior performance, using illustrative examples of how the best performers inside and outside your organization approach the tasks.

☑ Make jobs more playable; streamline processes; see how jobs fit together.

☑ Build on the standards, tying into a total system knowledge, skill, attitude, and recognition.

☑ Recognize various levels of performance—good, better, best.

☑ Create a ladder of accomplishment. Keep raising standards. Expect continuous improvement.

☑ Use standards to help assure consistent quality.

☑ Allow local flexibility; differentiate between principles and practices.

Apply the Learning

Break your own job down into written performance standards. Evaluate your performance against these standards. When you are confident of method and measurements, involve your bosses. Describe how you have rounded out the position, made it bigger and better-connected to what is important to the marketplace.

8

Develop a Curriculum That Teaches What Is Important

Do not simply become architects of facts; try to penetrate the secret of their occurrence, and persistently search for the laws which govern them.   ANONYMOUS

Businesses Need Curricula

When you are in an airplane, you hope the pilot has a body of knowledge and skill not just to take off, cruise, and land, but also to cope with unexpected conditions.

If you go too far out in the ocean and yell for a lifeguard, you hope that whoever is swimming your way has the capabilities to accomplish a result: to get you back to shore safely.

In business, when you count on other people, when, via the setting of standards and other strategic steps, you are clear on what you want workers to know, do, and feel, it is important that they be given the tools they need to succeed. It is the manager's opportunity as well as obligation to help them. The key thing for managers to remember is that training is not just something you buy anymore. It's something they and their people do together.

A curriculum is an instructional plan. It is based on the body of knowledge a person needs to meet the standards—and the responsibilities—of a task. This is true whether the standards are clearly specified, as described in Chapter 7, or implied through the smiles and frowns of bosses. The word curriculum derives from the Latin *currere*, to run a course or a race. A course of study or training is a disciplined and carefully designed structure of learning experiences to help an individual progress along a systematically determined career path.

Curriculum— A Management Tool

Curriculum design is more than the preparation of lessons. It is a valuable management tool. Organizational training, and therefore curricula, have to be tightly linked to the real world of day-to-day operations—what really constitutes success. Managers at every level of the organization must involve themselves in curriculum design so that the instruction revolves around what is truly important—no more, no less.

Earlier chapters discussed the importance of getting commitments *from* the people you are counting on to execute the change mandate. A well-defined curriculum is one of the most meaningful ways to demonstrate an organization's commitment *to* its people. It is thus central to forging a long-term productivity partnership, because everybody wins. Bosses gain the right to demand more without creating resentment because the assistance to achieve more is in place. Thus increased expectations are realistic and fair. Employees gain because they are being stretched to their full potential. They work in an organization where becoming all you can be is a way of life. They get to experience the exhilaration of new mastery.

Figure 8-1 illustrates the function of curriculum in an organization. To the productivity partnership, the organization brings expectations, policies, principles, resources, and a willingness to make decisions. The individual brings capabilities, interests, potentials, and initiatives.

From the context of business strategies, you define successful performances. You decide which elements of success depend upon knowledge, skill, and attitudes.

- Knowledge is the theoretical base for what must be mastered. It includes an explanation of events and presents models of conduct.

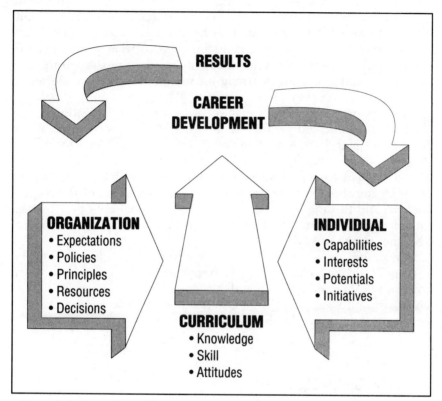

Figure 8-1. A sound curriculum is part of partnership.

- Skill development is the process of demonstrating that mastery in practice.
- Attitudinal factors address why the individual should do what is asked.

The curriculum brings the help that provides career development for the individual and results for the organization.

Tie the Curriculum to Business Goals

When participating in curriculum design, managers enjoy a powerful advantage. They have an inside view of what it takes to win. They have greater access to knowledge of what matters to customers. They have access to the strategic steps, such as the ones discussed in Part 1, including the setting of standards, and they have the day-to-day responsibility of explaining business requirements in terms of what people need to do, i.e., performance requirements. In short, managers are in the best position to make sure that learning for the job is directly connected to success.

That opportunity is frittered away in too many organizations by an ad hoc, disconnected jumble of advice and abortive assists. Every business organization has a body of knowledge that relates to success. There is always a curriculum in your business, whether it is known or not. The pain for employees and bosses alike is finding it, picking through the clutter of the unimportant, the confusion of the contradictory, and the anguish of receiving "instructional episodes" by trial and error, often preceded by the stern corrective admonishment, "No, no, not that way."

Curriculum development should not revolve around what trainers, managers, or consultants feel like imparting or even what the work force would like to know more about. A good business curriculum revolves around what people in a task need to do to be consistently successful, as determined by the marketplace.

Success by Design

Instructional design is an emerging specialty today, taught in a number of universities. While, like many specialties, there is a unique vocabulary, what instructional designers do parallels the thinking process of any logical manager. They follow a development path that asks the right questions and addresses the right issues in a structured and systemic way.

Pretesting to Save Trainee Time

Precisely stated objectives help adult trainees to step forward and identify when, through their life experience, knowledge and skill are already in place. This can be easily confirmed through pretesting. Pretests help your people concentrate on what is important and thus develop their potentials in the shortest possible time.

Communicating Learning Objectives

Because self-management is so important to productivity, make sure participants understand the relevance of each curriculum element and appreciate how the learning methods work together.

Sequencing Material for Maximum Payout

Curriculum design doesn't just help you decide what to offer but how to sequence it. It is important for the succession of activities to have logic and coherence. But the logic doesn't have to be pedantic and theoretical. In business, you sequence the flow of learning to teach what is most important first. What is most important is what makes the biggest difference to results, as defined by you, the manager. The closer learning is tailored to reflect how the knowledge and skill will be used on the job, the greater the chances of the material being put to use.

Figure 8-2 shows a practical way to organize the development of a body of learning:

- Establish performance standards based on targeted results.
- Analyze job tasks.
- Communicate learning objectives.
- Via tutorials, present the conceptual base. Show what you want and why.
- Share the experience of others, via examples and discussion.
- Provide opportunities to practice acquired skills.
- Use pretesting and posttesting to accelerate and validate progress.

Building in a Vision of Excellence

No manager has to settle for "what is." Teach "what ought to be." Teach excellence, not just current methods. If you are updating your curriculum, extend your thinking to new work practices that would make more of a difference in your marketplace. Test these practices in pilot activities and incorporate them into what you teach.

If the curriculum represents your organization's definition of success, it is very important that senior strategists as well as line managers insert

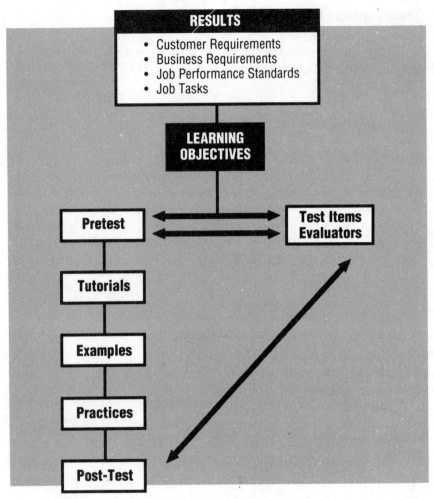

Figure 8-2. Model for organizing a training unit.

into curriculum design visionary definitions capable of yielding market-place advantage.

Making the Curriculum Complete

Mastery of the curriculum will lead to mastery of the real-world success elements of any given job. That's the quid pro quo for the tough job of learning new and better ways of doing things. That's why it's important that the curriculum be complete and sufficient to carry out that implied promise. Training or retraining is hard work. Learners must feel that the effort will yield a real return. Some organizations with catalogs full of "assists" have developed a reputation for "management by anecdote." A stray remark by a dealer, distributor, customer, or boss—or the latest fad—sends the organization off on a short-lived tangent. A flurry of activity produces "one more job-development course." When such randomness and impulsiveness are part of business training, employees become reluctant participants. They feel cheated when material they have worked hard to master turns out not to be mainstream to their real world.

Making Decisions Easier and Faster

Without a curriculum map, decisions regarding what to teach next become harder than they need to be.

A committee supervising a long-term effort to build sales professionalism was floundering. Executives representing many different units of the company couldn't agree on next steps. An outside business-education consultant's recommendations seemed too theoretical. Confusion reigned. Then one frustrated operating executive, tired of the circular conversation, seized the crayon and the chart stand. This pragmatist put aside all of the fancy documents, turned to a fresh, blank page, and asked fellow executives one question: "Based on your operating experience, what do our outstanding sales people *do* to be successful?" The group made a list of task specifics. When the managers returned to their deliberations on course assistance, they quickly matched the needs against existing resources and circled the gaps. The next steps became clear very quickly and with a lot less pain.

Creating a Loop for Ongoing Enrichment

Because business is dynamic, the curriculum should be dynamic too and should, therefore, be continually updated. A business curriculum is like a bank account. Participants not only make "withdrawals." A well-designed organizational curriculum gives them an understanding of a total body of knowledge and a disciplined developmental process. When they go back on the job after any training module, they should be encouraged to make "deposits" to "their" curriculum to help those who follow them. So long-term linkages should be established for learners to add their own experiences and variations on concepts. In that way, concepts can be continually modified and amplified with the techniques of

emerging master performers to meet changing marketplace requirements, and the company's experience base is continually enriched.

Positive Side-Effects of
Strategic Curriculum Building

A Tool for Recruiting and Bonding

Establishing a curriculum tied to career development indicates a commitment that can be a powerful recruiting tool. The intelligent, caring
people who represent the cream of the nation's labor pool want to join
companies that are committed to the growth of people. A curriculum
tied to a career plan represents clear thinking and organizational commitment to human potential. Introducing the curriculum plan, with examples of your course offerings, into recruiting conversations as a
source of company pride provides an edge with thinking prospects.

A Tool for Turnover-Proofing Your
Organization

Competitors and others would like to attract your best people. Every job
has frustrations and low points—times of vulnerability to the entice-
ments of other jobs. When a company has a curriculum that leads to
career growth and a number of executives share the learning experience, alumni become a valuable organizational resource. The learning
process is more than facts, figures, and information. The open-minded
curiosity that learning stimulates is also a time when friendships and
loyalties are formed. Arrange alumni social events, brief refresher updates, and other activities to strengthen these bonds.

Conclusion: Fostering a Sense
of Wonder

A young child coming home after her first day in kindergarten remarks, "I learned some things I didn't understand. And then I learned
to understand them." That same wide-eyed curiosity of the young is
something that must be preserved and nurtured in adult training. The
most important part of education is learning to learn.

In a business setting, it's important that the learner feel that help is in
place to grow and to meet standards—help that is practical, directly applicable to the real world, and truly market-oriented.

The curriculum is a reservoir of relevant knowledge and skills. It's a
source for specially tailored courses, which can be broken down further

into units of learning. And it provides standards and evaluators for testing for formal or informal certification of users.

When employees feel that the curriculum is tailored not only to the tasks...but to them personally, then an attachment forms for lifelong development and change, and they feel comfortable depositing their own best practices for future reference by others.

A contemporary curriculum is more than a set of courses. In a world of pressures, challenges, heavy competition, and frustration, a well-planned curriculum leading to growth becomes a resource, a friend, and one more element in the partnership for productivity.

Checklist for Change

☑ Tie the curriculum directly to business goals and performance standards.

☑ Update the curriculum to meet changing times.

☑ Follow practical instructional design principles.

☑ Pretest to save learner time.

☑ Make the learning complete—the knowledge, skill, and attitude requisites for success.

☑ Sequence material logically for maximum payout.

☑ Use methods that motivate interest and stimulate real-world use.

☑ Continually enrich the curriculum with pilot activities, experience "deposits," best practices, and feedback.

☑ Use the curriculum for recruiting, coaching, personalized development, and bonding.

Apply the Learning

Take one skill important to your success or the growth of a subordinate. Develop a curriculum plan to address that skill, clarifying what you should teach and how you should teach it. Compare this to how you learned the skill and what is currently available to others. Look for improvements you can act on, gaps in the assistance available to you and others.

9

Apply the Power of Information Technology

You can send a message around the world in one-seventh of a second, yet it may take years to move a simple idea through a quarter-inch of human skull.   CHARLES F. KETTERING

Look Before You Leap into Expensive Investment in Technology

Technology and Turf

Today, technology is sweeping across organizational lines, threatening the status quo of people, departments, and operations. Electronic networks rearrange the frequency, content, and flow of information throughout big companies. Specific data and information become more accessible to larger numbers of people. In corporations, as everywhere else, knowledge is power. So electronic technology is altering the real power lines and power bases in many organizations.

Managers are frequently troubled by this trend, even though they may be excited by the possibilities. They see the benefits to the company but also often see threats to themselves or their traditional turfs. This ambiguous reaction, while very human, can slow the process by which

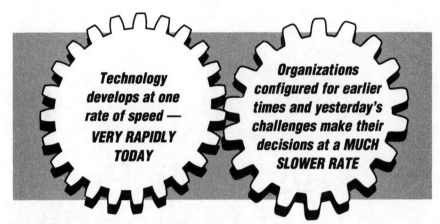

Figure 9-1. Technological changes are occurring more rapidly than the ability of organizations to comprehend and decide.

technology becomes a legitimate and reliable partner in productivity. (See Figure 9.1.)

So, Charles Kettering, scientist, engineer, and inventor, put his finger on the dilemma of seizing the potential of technology. The technical issues are easy compared to the human issues.

While individualized training and retraining can be accomplished in a formal classroom setting, with support as low-tech as chalk and a chalkboard, prescriptiveness in business learning gets powerful impetus today from the rapid advances and interactive potential of learning and information technology. The very speed with which these advances have occurred has outpaced the ability of many organizations to coherently address and respond to the issues.

When it comes to technology, the first question asked in organizations often seems to be, Which new hardware system should we buy for our branches, franchise locations, or learning centers? That question is premature when such underlying issues as authority, responsibility, strategy, customer-satisfaction requirements, clear-cut performance standards, total curriculum, and career-path development have not first been addressed. The preceding chapters helped put questions about the application of technology into a logical context.

Of all the partnerships for productivity, one of the most important and challenging to establish is the partnership between people charged with producing goods and services, the information/learning communication devices that can enlarge human potential, and the people who create and understand these tools.

This chapter focuses on the evaluation of technology, not as isolated, free-standing equipment choices, but in a different, future-oriented context as everyday extensions of how people perform such common business functions as managing, deciding, selling, explaining, learning, and other aspects of their work. There are three overriding considerations for technology-application decision making:

1. *Implications:*   Make every effort to see the possibilities on a timely basis, evaluate the technological alternatives and solutions systematically, apply when ready—not too late and not too soon.

2. *Integration:*   Tie together your various investments in information processing and get them in harmony with how the value-added work in your operation is really done.

3. *Impact* on the organization: Create receptivity to continuing, dynamic change in responsibilities, power, and influence.

Getting in Sync with Technological Opportunities and Options

Companies are littered with technology mistakes:

- Choices made too early or too late because decision makers didn't adequately grasp what was coming.

- Information machines that do not talk to each other and may even contradict.

- Investments made and systems introduced with a human receptivity factor far different than envisioned.

When powerful new technology comes along, most business leaders believe they'll recognize it for sure. But how certain can you be? Consider, for example, Figure 9-2, a letter from the chairman of a nineteenth-century "technology evaluation committee."

A Compendium of Missed Opportunities

There are innumerable examples of lag time in grasping the implications of emerging technologies. When Marconi invented radio, the only uses envisioned were point-to-point communication of information, sort of a "spoken" telegraph key. The whole tapestry of radio entertainment was not foreseen. It came about through experimentation. Even after radio became the focus of home entertainment in the 1930s and early 1940s, immediately following World War II, FM radio stations could be purchased for bargain prices. Many communications industry executives believed that television would make radio obsolete. Fortunes were made by bargain hunters who recognized that radio's economy and portability would allow it to thrive in happy coexistence with television.

November 15, 1876
President, Western Union Telegraph Company

...Messrs. Hubbard and Bell want to install one of their "telephone" devices in virtually every home and business establishment in the city. This idea is idiotic on the face of it. Furthermore, why would any person want to use this ungainly and impractical device when he can send a messenger to the local telegraph office and have a clear written message sent to any large city in the United States?

The electricians of your own company have developed all the significant improvements in the telegraph art to date, and we see no reason why a group of outsiders, with extravagant and impractical ideas, should be entertained when they have not the slightest idea of the true practical problems involved. Mr. G. G. Hubbard's fanciful predictions, while they sound very rosy, are based upon wild-eyed imaginations and a lack of understanding of the technical and economic factors of the situation, and a posture of ignoring the obvious technical limitations of his device, which is hardly more than a toy, or a laboratory curiosity...

...Mr. G. G. Hubbard's request for $100,000 for the sale of this patent is utterly unreasonable, since the device is inherently of no value to us. We do not recommend the purchase.

Figure 9-2.

Around Christmastime, 1947, a team at Bell Laboratories invented the transistor. Four years later, the parent company, AT&T, put up the nonexclusive rights for sale for $25,000. One of the purchasers of that license to use transistors was Sony in Japan, which promptly became the world leader in transistor radios. Sony's flexibility and imagination can be illustrated by the story of a failed R&D effort. Sony's chairman was getting bad news about a product development that was not materializing. Although disappointed, the chief became fascinated with the earphones he was using to listen to the results. He encouraged development of those test earphones, and they became one of the most successful commercial product lines of the twentieth century, the Sony Walkman.[9]

The book *Fumbling the Future* tells the distressing story of how Xerox set up, superbly staffed, and liberally funded a West Coast think tank on the future of computing and other information technologies. But Xerox's senior managers didn't realize what they had. They didn't appreciate or act on the possibilities.[10]

Xerox, AT&T, and other high-tech companies are filled with executives who live on the leading edge of technological advancement. If these people make such mistakes, how is the average manager to gain a sense of the implications of new methods?

1. By making the usefulness of technology to people needs your frame of reference.

2. By making the role of technology in the overall work process your context.

3. By making the creation of tools for people to be more productive the consistent goal.

The Benefits of Prescriptive Technologies

The kinds of prescriptive technologies described in this chapter are beneficial because they respond to the challenges of the information glut and the preferences of adult-level learners in a variety of ways. Understanding the implications of information technology puts managers in a better position to:

- *Move the learning closer to the learner.*   The office, store, or other work site, the home, even the automobile, can now be considered advanced learning centers.

- *Allow the learner to pace his or her own development.*   Branching permits pushing past what is already known to what is fresh and new.

- *Demand active learning.*   The mind has to be in gear. If you are part of a carpool that takes you to the same destination for 20 years, and if you are never behind the wheel making active choices, you won't easily find the way by yourself. A person learns when challenged to make decisions. Action learning puts the emphasis on the *application* of what you are learning.

- *Test frequently.*   Responses are called for to make sure the learner is truly absorbing the material.

- *Provide practical, simple access.*   Users do not have to learn a complex computer language. They make choices from a menu of items. In the not-too-distant future, users will be able through voice-activated technology to talk directly to these automated "tutors," telling them real-world operating problems, like closing a sale, getting out of a slump, performing a specific repair function, or explaining the true meaning of small-print contract terms. Simply voicing the problem will bring up a screen that will assist with solutions.

- *Start development immediately.*   With prescriptive technologies in place, a new hire can start learning immediately without having to wait for classes to form.

- *Coach prescriptively.*   A business associate can be sent over to a work station to gain knowledge or skill on a precise weakness or need as soon as the need is perceived.

- *Allow greater privacy and comfort levels.*   Adults feel vulnerable when they don't know something that they should. This is a time when interacting with an impersonal machine can preserve dignity.

- *Administer carefully.*   Interactive learning machines can automatically keep track of course work completed as students take tests or log-off the equipment.

- *Give timely feedback.*   The scoring and administrative features provide an important yield—information regarding use, mastery, difficulty of segments, and other important evaluations.

- *Assure consistency.*   Getting improved performance that your customers can count on depends upon *consistency*. Technology-based prescriptive learning teaches at the same level—every day, every student, every time.

- *Save time and money.*   When there is a critical mass of trainees and knowledge, development costs are rapidly recovered.

User Experiences

As testimony to the effectiveness of high-tech solutions to training needs, consider the following cases:

Xerox saves $6 million each year by training 15,000 field service technicians with interactive videodiscs. Taking into account the cost of travel and lost work time, Xerox estimates that it saves $300 to $600 per trainee each day. They conclude that interactive videodisc reduces training time by 30 percent and increases the learning rate by 40 percent.

Massachusetts Mutual Life Insurance Company reports a 40 percent increase in sales productivity and a 50 percent reduction in training time by use of a hardware combination of touch-screen monitors, laser disc players, personal computers, and video camera/recorders for role-playing.[11]

Prudential Life Insurance reports that its agents' pass rate—those who satisfactorily master the work—moved from 68 percent via lectures to almost 90 percent via computer-based instruction.

IBM is moving its billion-dollar-plus training investments from 75 percent classroom/25 percent individualized instruction to about 50 percent individualized instruction today, heading toward 75 percent.

Scandinavian Air Systems (SAS) converted a two-day cabinet attendant course to a visual, self-paced format. They found they could compress the course to *one hour.*

Profile of the Latest in Interactive Technologies

There are machines that have the characteristics of a wise and patient tutor. In addition, they have the power to harness and combine two important technologies:

- The visual power of television or other clarifying graphics
- The customized information-retrieval capabilities of the computer

As power, resolution, speed, portability, and cost-effectiveness increase, interactive training technologies become more and more available, useful, and affordable.

A primary example of interactive training technology is the laser videodisc. Combining television and computer, it offers up to 54,000 still frames of data on one record plus full video motion plus multiple audio tracks. The videodisc allows the user precise, instant retrieval and branching to what he or she needs to know the most about. In an interactive learning situation, such as how to service an appliance, the videodisc is set up so that incorrect answers trigger the branching, taking the student to material that has not yet been mastered but needs to be.

The now-common VCR, with its recording capability, also can be programmed for interactive learning, but retrieval lacks the speed and precision of the videodisc.

Interactive video today is being used by over 11 percent of organizations to deliver training. These investments represent about 2 percent of total training expenditures. That share is headed toward a very significant 8 percent of dollars invested by 1992.

The personal computer has become omnipresent. There are 40 million personal computers in offices, stores, and homes today, and the population of personal computers is growing by 6 million a year. These are capable of far more than word processing, spreadsheets, or data collection. The important frontier for computerized information, whether free-standing or tied to interactive television, is as knowledge centers.

Computer-based instruction today is being used by over 44 percent of organizations and represents about 30 percent of total training investments. Not only is the personal computer widely available, but computer-based instruction teaches about a third faster than live, stand-up instruction.

Trends such as computer work stations and HDTV (high-definition television) with sharper images will vastly increase the capabilities of prescriptive learning centers.

The headlong drive to combine the informational capabilities of computers and the power of video is moving rapidly into its next stages. The two movements to watch can be summarized by the initials DVI (digital video interactive) and CDI (compact disc interactive).

As recently reported in the *Wall Street Journal*: "There have been many scattershot efforts to mesh PCs and video, but these two projects could hit the mark, because they are backed by the world's most important standard setters for home and office electronics."[12]

- DVI can put video and photography into a personal computer. Intel Corporation is developing a set of microchips that can compress an hour of video on a compact disc. Owners of next generation IBM PCs will be able to put a card with DVI chips into the backs of their computers and view television in one corner of the screen while using the rest of the screen for information, analysis, and input.

- CDI uses a CD player which plugs into a television set. The developer, N. V. Phillips, is aiming at the broad consumer market as well as business.

Prescriptive learning will continue to gain in simplicity and economy as the same mass production know-how that has made the compact audio disc so popular is applied to televised learning. Compact disc interactive technology, using the same 4¾-inch disc used in home stereo systems, can hold as much information as 1500 floppy discs.

Technologies like these, and others to come, can be considered as alternatives to the traditional paths into the minds of employees.

Software, Groupware, Transactionware, and Performanceware

It is well understood today that even the most sophisticated technology can achieve no more than the quality of the software. But the nature of software is changing as rapidly as the hardware, as the following statement from a recent *Newsweek* article suggests:

> In the future, no computer will be an island...there will be a new class of software: "groupware." Groupware will stimulate collaboration, will change the way work is done. For example, firms are testing calendar systems that automatically set up meetings by going through the network to ask each person's computer when the individual has free time.

As computers and other technologies become increasingly integral to how people work, learn, and receive information, a distinction also needs to be made between "transactionware" and "performanceware."

Spreadsheets, word processing, and many other useful tools deal with transactions. Experts in business objectives and processes meet with experts in technology and together, develop new procedures, reports, and other forms of useful transactionware.

Performanceware wraps around the transactionware, but addresses additional dimensions, potentials, and needs:

- How is the work performed, and how could it be performed more productively and with greater usefulness and value for customers, external and internal? Giving a priority to real-world uses by human beings in the marketplace can very well trigger a different structure of information. For example, computerized product information might best be organized for retrieval in the structured sequences that sales people use to sell the product to customers.
- What other information is available from other sources? How can these various reports be merged?
- How can people learn as they use the tools? We have discussed self-paced, computer-based instruction and its growing role in all kinds of training. Performanceware refers to the integration of learning steps with the transactional use of the tools: learn-as-you-go.

Continuous Scanning and Cycle Times

The keys to seeing implications on a timely basis include:

- *Scanning continuously.* Technologies keep changing.
- *Seeing the patterns to cycle times*—the time it takes to move ideas to proven assists.
- *Looking at investment in training and information technology as consumable marketing and productivity investment,* not as long-term fixed assets. Advanced technology is like a continually curving road ahead. You can usually see something even better coming along. You make investments in information technology when, for a reasonable period, you can calculate improvements in human performance, customer satisfaction, and business methods sufficient to pay for the investment plus a profit.

When an organization delays or compromises too long, it can be costly to find and uproot the consequences. What you put into the mind isn't easily expunged. Here's a way to think about it.

Let's say an educated immigrant moves to New York City but can't initially afford either fine furniture or fine language education. So he compromises on both. He buys a cheap sofa with poor springs and ugly upholstery. And he takes English lessons from a kid off the streets who teaches him how to say "foist" for first, "thoid" for third, "brudda" for brother, and other words unique to the street world. Time passes. Fortunes improve. The newcomer can now easily discard the sofa and buy better furniture. But it will be a painful process now to learn the language of the nation rather than of one city's streets.

While this example is exaggerated, it simply illustrates the cost in pain and frustration when corporations dump inappropriate and irrelevant material into the minds of their people, using interim packages of "available stuff" until the organization has time to think through what their people really need in these times.

Knowing when to make long-run commitments to advanced methods depends upon truly knowing where you are in the development cycle. The U.S. Department of Labor and the American Society for Training and Development offer the following four-phase sequence as a broad outline of the typical course of cycle time:

- The discovery or development of a technical innovation
- The tailoring of the innovation to the institutional culture, strategic niche, and production or service station

- Widespread use of the innovation
- The development of new applications

Integrate Information
Elements Based upon Need

A branch manager sits at the kitchen table on a Sunday evening, a variety of computer reports spread out before him. In this age of rapid information dissemination, he is plying a craft as old as the scripting of ancient monks. With a heavy black crayon, he is painstakingly putting key figures onto chart pages and transparencies so that he can review trends Monday morning in a way that will have meaning to the people he supervises. What a gain in productivity it would represent if in the first place his company's computers portrayed information in the way team members really use it.

When you consider new methods of disseminating information, as with people skills, inventory what is already in place. Look at all your existing information technologies together. Consider how these hardware and software capabilities match up against your people requirements, skills, and gaps. Otherwise you run the risk of proliferating overlapping or even contradictory information flows.

- Begin with customer requirements, business strategies, and performance standards.
- Focus on what you want your people to know and to do.
- Analyze all the ways that individuals learn and receive information in your company.

When you conduct that kind of analysis, you may be surprised not only by the volume of information flows but also by the degree of inconsistency. Reports, tools, meetings, video reports, rankings, and the like, are often developed by different groups at different times with different formats.

Integrating tools becomes even more important as a corporation's computer power increases, networks emerge, and linkages are established directly with customers, branches, and franchise locations.

An Important Choice—To
Informate or Automate

In her milestone work, *In the Age of the Smart Machine—The Future of Work and Power*, Professor Shoshana Zuboff of Harvard Business

School discusses the implications of technologies that can "informate" as well as automate.

- To automate involves telling the machine to perform the task. For repetitive functions, the worker needs to know less.

- To informate involves programming so that the equipment can also communicate what it is doing, making processes visible and transparent. This makes information that has traditionally been private, the province of a managerial elite, widely available. What human beings *do* with this information is the high-yield part of technology.

Zuboff points out that informating and automating are profoundly different strategies, requiring different skills and presenting significantly different work experiences.[13] Beneath the surface, she warns, are dilemmas and potential collisions over the future of work and power:

- Who will know? (Information that matters.)
- Who will decide who will know?
- What will the criteria be for these choices?
- How much/how fast can/should the organization be changed to take advantage of the new potentials?

Unfortunately, managers often become defensive about the widespread distribution of knowledge and power. Hierarchies and functional boundaries can subtly retard the process of human liberation that is attainable. Managers are normally protected by walls of people and paper. Wide access to information means that the collector won't "own" the data anymore. Real ownership of information moves to those who understand the implications and use the data to add value to every step of the work process.

Whether or not an organization makes changes in structure, when technology comes to the work site, learning priorities shift. Thinking and learning to learn become more important.

It is not the questions themselves but the willingness to question and the process of inquiry that are important today. Answers will differ by company, industry, or nation.

Conclusion: The Stakes Are Getting Higher

There is more at stake here than just making the "most efficient use of the computer over there in the corner." Consider some of these recent trends in technology:

- Corporations set up sophisticated telemarketing centers to conduct business on a daily basis with field locations.

- Live satellite connects headquarters to branch stores with the immediacy of live television broadcasting.

- Customers and employees use toll-free telephone lines for assistance and complaint resolution.

- Field representatives carry lightweight lap-top computers and VCRs for order entry and product demonstration.

- Retail selling environments as well as offices become rich in available computerized information.

Whenever information dissemination becomes central to how the affairs of a business are conducted, the training function can no longer be looked at as a disconnected experience.

Only when functional specialists can be persuaded to lessen loyalty to craft and turf and take a true team perspective regarding the success of the total organization will the opportunities be fully realized. The organizational choices would be less daunting if they could be approached slowly. But it's like jumping a chasm: you need a bold, confident leap. Applying technology intelligently forces you to take a fresh look at processes, to see the organization clearly and as a whole—what is and what could be.

Checklist for Change

☑ Understand the implications of emerging technologies and widely distributed information as the transforming resources of our time.

☑ Make the usefulness to people your frame of reference. Evaluate benefits of prescriptive technologies, such as time savings and self-paced and active learning.

☑ Understand developmental cycles so you can judge when to make best use of new technologies.

☑ Look at technological investments as consumable business costs, not as long-term assets. Move ahead when you can get enough gains in performance to show a profit.

☑ Integrate technologies so that information streams, reports, courses, organizational communication activities, and management practices reinforce consistent messages and teachings.

☑ Anticipate the impact on the organization—how technology can transform work, power, and influence. Work to achieve a team perspective that breaks down turf walls.

Apply the Learning

Take one or several computerized reports or other information packages that cross your desk. Trace where they originate and where else they go. Take a look at who uses them, how they could be combined, how they could be made more effective, more timely, more relevant at a human interaction point—that is, when somebody meets the customer, when functions hand off from one person to another, or when courseware is being developed.

10

Use Media for Learning as a Window to See Anywhere

This instrument, television, can teach; it can illuminate; yes, it can even inspire. But it can do so only to the extent that humans are determined to use it to those ends. Otherwise, it is merely wires and lights in a box.
                    EDWARD R. MURROW

Cut Through Media Proliferation

Americans buy 62 million newspapers a day. They spend an average of 6 hours a day with the television set on, tune in to 10,500 radio stations for over 3 hours a day, choose from 11,500 magazines and 3000 computer databases. 190 million prerecorded videocassettes are manufactured in the United States each year. Americans use the telephone more than 3700 trillion minutes per year. Automatic dialers can ring as many as 20,000 phone numbers a day with unsolicited sales calls. Two to three million messages a day go out via electronic mail. Fax machines are being installed at the rate of 150,000 per month. That's information, entertainment, and education on a massive scale.

Through all the sights and sounds that surround us also come the voices of family, bosses, colleagues, customers, friends, and neighbors. Impressions come from many directions. The latest joke, fact, or instruction enters your mind from somewhere. It's hard to remember from where or when.

The good news is that media is becoming dramatically less expensive, faster, and easier to produce. The bad news is that by being less expensive, faster, and easier to produce, media is becoming omnipresent. When chosen carelessly or implemented impulsively, media bounces off the eyes and ears as just more noise pollution. Defenses arise. The video remote control zapper becomes an indispensable household implement, a weapon for obliterating at least some of the messages that clamor for our attention.

The sights and sounds that permeate our lives can be more than diversionary entertainment, more than straight information transfer. Media today is a management tool—a way to learn, teach, communicate, monitor, persuade, motivate, and report.

Technology today permits us to teach Shakespeare more vividly, to recreate the tone and feel of the Vietnam war, to get inside the human body and travel through the bloodstream. It can also be profitably used to display the expertise, the uniqueness, the needs of any business organization in equally dramatic and powerful ways.

Media is the plural of *medium*, a channel or system of communication, information, or entertainment. This chapter looks at media from the education-action perspective. Ways are discussed to move educational assistance closer to the work site. Some of the same concepts can help you add visual punch to your next report, access information more efficiently, anticipate trends, and make better choices in how you learn and teach others.

Performance Improvement vs. Entertainment Applications

In working for human performance improvement, we use information and entertainment, but the target lies beyond that. The point is to change situations, attitudes, and behaviors.

Business communication is often wrapped in entertainment and showmanship, but it should not be confused with pure entertainment. Entertainment and business communication part company on their objectives. Entertainment strives for applause. Business communication should strive for action. It should have a purposeful intelligence, a focus on what happens afterwards. And that takes intense concentration on what you want people to know, do, and feel after the message has been delivered. While content is an important part of training media, the objective is not simply to add to the supply of information but to present actionable information that is acted upon in ways directly related to success.

In business applications, media is often applied as a substitute for travel to a central location. Learning can be moved closer to the learner. The book *The Media Lab*, about research at MIT, calls media "our longest arm"—a way to reach people. Media gives access to "another mind." That is, it's a way to make available other people's experiences.[14]

Business media is often segmented for use in workplace settings with the lights up. Rather than the linear emotional experience of the darkened movie palace, business media illuminates and clarifies key points. Sequences are to be called upon as needed, in partnership with customers, suppliers, or employees. Television, for example, can be used as a window rather than as a stage. Through the window, millions of people can simultaneously see, hear, and "feel" events, often as they happen. Applying television to productivity improvement, we can teach master performance, for example, and send TV cameras anywhere in the world to show what we mean—repeatedly, and in slow motion, if we wish. Entertainers use television as a stage upon which to perform. Educators apply television as a way to extend vision—to see and visit best practices, wherever they may be found.

Business communication develops its wallop differently from entertainment. John DeLorean was a flamboyant, show-biz-minded general manager at Chevrolet. Married to a beautiful young actress, he made it a practice to select major Hollywood entertainment studios to produce new-product-introduction motion pictures for his dealer organization. One particularly difficult year, DeLorean's executive team also staged a series of candid 6-hour new-product briefings for dealers at GM's Tech Center Design Dome. In plain-speaking, hard-hitting language, competitive challenges were faced, future directions portrayed, and product advantages demonstrated. The dealers were appreciative.

When, a few days after participating in these briefings, DeLorean went to California to review his lavishly produced Hollywood epic, which was supposed to have been aimed at dealership sales managers and sales people who hadn't come to Detroit, he was startled to find little of the content and none of the power of the Tech Center briefings. The developers of the Tech Center event were invited to "open up" the glossy Hollywood epic and insert "business content." In business, impact comes from content, not just beautiful imagery.

One thing that business and entertainment communication do share is that they both play to the audience. A live audience gives immediate feedback. A receptive audience channels energy back into a presentation.

When used for business performance improvement, media should be considered as pathways into the mind to achieve follow-up action. This is substantially different from using media for pure entertainment or for raw information transfer.

Media Selection for Productivity

Precision in selecting the most effective media is as important as precision in the content of the message. No one medium is right for every purpose or person. Each has a distinctive advantage. If any one method were superior in every dimension—speed, cost, portability, duplication, and impact—it would carry the day and all other ways would disappear. It's similar to the reason for having a range of clubs in a golf bag. Each one is designed for a specific purpose. So you make trade-offs based upon your specific business objectives.

And you make trade-offs based upon your employees' different learning styles. In human performance terms, media represent alternative routes into the mind—alternatives to one-on-one instruction, meetings, seminars, memos, manuals, megaphones, and repetitive orders. Because different people receive information in different ways, each of the media forms, or various combinations of them, can profitably be used to improve the receptivity of organizational messages.

As powerful as TV is, many people prefer to learn through printed material, which is less expensive, more portable, and can be read or re-read anywhere at almost any time. Television and print together, obviously, can produce a more powerful instructional effect than either alone.

In making media selections, consider criteria such as the following:

- *Impact:* using the full emotional and clarifying power of the communication.
- *Speed:* getting information rapidly distributed and used.
- *Interactivity:* talking back, asking questions, working with the media proactively in the same way you collaborate with a dynamic associate or a teacher or coach.
- *Retrievability:* accessing the material when you want to refresh yourself or use the information on the job.

- *Economy:*   getting the most value for the dollars and time expended.

Achieving Visual Impact

With the proliferation of visual communication, there is particular need to strive for impact and memorability, to carefully develop the striking image that changes forever the way we think about things. You achieve impact in business communication through:

- Skillful application of the arts of sight and sound
- Imagination
- Relevance of content

Consider, for example, how the following television images have transformed the way we look at the world:

Image	*Theme*
Southern sheriff Bull Connor and his bulldogs	Human rights
Presidential funeral of John F. Kennedy	Shared grief
View of planet earth from the moon	Human vulnerability, concern for the environment
One million Chinese student protesters in the square at Beijing	More voice by the people governed
George Bush television commercials of pollution in Boston harbor	Defining Presidential campaign issues

In developing "sound bites" politicians and other newsmakers as well as advertisers have found that the repetition of a single carefully planned visual that goes to the essence of an issue has a powerful impact.

The same principle applies to organizational communication and education. Instead of thousands of words or lazy images, managers stand to benefit by being alert to how product advantages and business methods can be vividly summarized by the crystallizing image that sticks in the mind. In a world that learns visually, contemporary managers who continually look around for evidence of superiority and express it visually will have the advantage. There are steps in everyday product development, testing, and transactional processes that could prove advantageous in believable ways. Get in the habit of building a file, including Polaroid or other photos, of why and how your products or services are better.

If managers, who are closest to their businesses, bring such an array of possibilities to a creative discussion, audiovisual professionals bring a dazzling variety of interpretive enhancements. Leading-edge work today is heightening visual impact by combining film, video, computer, live photography, animation, and special effects material in a single frame of film. George Lucas's film, *Who Framed Roger Rabbit?*, not only combines live and cartoon characters but has a scene in which cartoon characteristics—carefully animated eyes of blazing intensity—are superimposed on the live actor.

The way to tell if your video and film communications have visual impact is to review them with the sound turned off. A strong visual sequence tells its story without words.

Consider, for example, the challenge of describing a truck that is slimmer than its major competitor, yet has more load capacity and a cargo bed height that is closer to the height of most loading docks. A "lazy" sequence might show this with routine visuals of a truck on a road. High-impact business photography would demonstrate the benefits of such a truck by showing the alley that will let one truck through but is too tight for the competitor, the cargo that will fit in one truck and not the other, the loading dock that permits easy-rolling cargo removal for one truck but not the other, and the consequences as truckers do their work. Business impact comes from a combination of careful visualization and pointing the camera at what has the most meaning to the business audience.

—World's fairs are frequently showcases for the new. At Expo '67 in Montreal, Johnson's Wax's "To Be Alive" was a smash hit and helped usher in the era of multiple images. Twenty years later, at the Vancouver World's Fair, those same kinds of multiple images were everywhere, but now were taken for granted. This time, General Motors of Canada stole the show with an Indian storyteller in front of a campfire. From the flames of that fire rose holographic images, quietly mystical in their depth and changing shapes.

—The claymation technique used for the famous dancing California Raisin television commercials is another example of achieving impact through unique visual methods. That technique earns high recall and will continue to do so while the imagery is new.

—Impact does not always depend upon great scale. Everyday props used at the right time can have visual power. Ray Ketchledge was president of Austin Rover Cars of North America and needed to get across to the board of the parent company in England that parts defects were excessive for such a luxury car as the Sterling. He could have just talked. Instead, he dumped out on the highly polished boardroom table a laundry bag full of defective parts.

Perspectives on Communication Speed

Live open lines—telephone, satellite television, computers, and fax machines—permit virtually immediate real-time communication. With express mail, other visual packages can reach users with remarkable speed. The key issue is to determine under what circumstances you need this kind of immediacy.

When you emphasize speed, you should simultaneously consider three separate elements:

- Speed in developing message content
- Speed in transmission
- Speed of those on the receiving end to understand and act on the information

When you look at all three elements of speed together, you put yourself in a position to make informed trade-offs. Another 100 hours to polish, clarify, and compress the communication might save thousands of viewer hours in comprehending and integrating the information.

The speed of communication revolves around *when the material is used*, not when it is shipped. Material prepared as part of a master curriculum and interpreted with painstaking visual craftsmanship over many months might represent the ultimate in rapid communication when it can be immediately accessed by an employee at the moment of need. Conversely, material rushed to users to be shoved into desk drawers because the issue is not on their agenda at that particular moment does not represent useful speed.

Live satellite television is coming into its own for situations in which both speed and impact are important. Private networks are springing up that can combine daily television programming and substantial data flow. There are almost 2 million receiving dishes on U.S. rooftops. It is feasible today to have communication networks that combine several technologies: for example, live satellite transmission for certain key locations, with express-mailed videocassettes to bring the same material to other locations a day later.

For continuous rapid communications, the organization should streamline its program development and decision processes. As time lags and distance barriers can be made to disappear, some other things must also disappear—excuses, the leisurely assembling of answers, and the fear of spontaneous human communication. Organizational communication today can be as rapid as you want, need, and will gear to accomplish.

How to Foster Interactivity

Live open lines such as satellite and telephone are ideal for two-way communication. But the questions aren't limited to the simple clarification of information. Those on the receiving end take a stronger hand in shaping the communication agenda by telling you what they want to know more about. One of the most important parts of productivity partnerships is to respond to what the listener wants and needs, not just what you choose to communicate. Be prepared to continually modify your programming to meet audience needs, not just organizational objectives. When you become serious about interactivity as mainstream communication learning and communication strategy, then methods such as live satellite television, classrooms, conference calls, interactive laser videodisc, and computer-based instruction become preferred methods.

How to Encourage Retrieval for Relevance

You want the full power of business learning and information retrieved when it is most relevant to the issues at hand. Printed materials and computer-based information and instruction are particularly useful for ready access. When you are choosing your methods in the context of longer-term strategy, it is possible to combine impact, speed, interactivity, and retrieval. For example, a big-screen 35mm motion picture in a theatre or as part of a big show can also be made easily retrievable in follow-up videocassette or printed recap formats.

Retrieval strategy includes emphasizing audiovisual equipment that is lightweight and portable, such as today's small, handy VCR television units and lap-top computers. It also means riding through the channels already in existence in an organization and its branches, independent dealers, and customer locations. When audiovisual hardware is already in place in a number of conference rooms, offices, stores, and even employee homes, then retrieval becomes much easier. It's old-fashioned and overly expensive to call people into meetings to receive information that they could look at, hear, or read when and where they need it.

Today's workplace, home, or car is frequently a well-equipped information center. Inventory what is out there. Use it. To standardize around certain television or computer formats, it can make very good economic sense for corporations to subsidize or completely underwrite the purchase of company-selected television and computer equipment for the home. Employees get a perk in state-of-the-art entertainment appliances. Employers put a straight, clear, dependable dissemination channel in place. That's a win-win partnership. Corporations get a significant return when employees are encouraged to use their own spare time to learn and stay current.

How to Be More Economical

The best economies in media selection are achieved through:

- Getting business results that pay for the production plus a profit
- Saving the time of the learner
- Setting clear specifications

Because the first two and other value-stretching techniques are taken up fully in Chapter 14, the concentration in this section is on setting media specifications.

A, B, and C Production Levels. The decisions of operating managers on media utilization don't simply involve what kind, but also what level of production to utilize.

The least expensive part of corporate media production today is the cost of the film, video, computer diskette, or paper stock. The most expensive decision is what you point the camera at:

- C level—Tell and imply.
- B level—Do more showing of what you mean.
- A level—Demonstrate a wider variety of applications, go to more locations, use a bigger cast and more special effects to explain and clarify.

You make these investment choices on the basis of the program environment and how the material will be used. The program environment not only influences production levels but the personality and character of the media use. There is a difference, for example, between a newspaper that emphasizes bowling scores and social news and a performance publication that uses realistic journalism to cover progress on

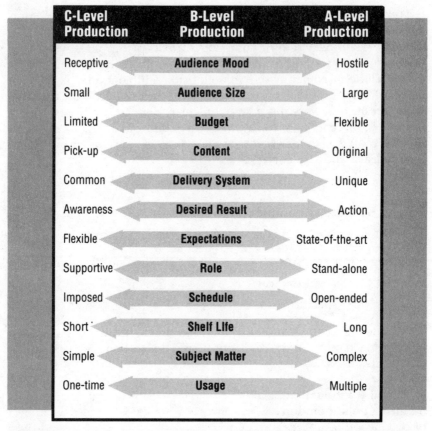

Figure 10-1. Program environment influences production levels. (*Source: Sandy Corporation.*)

carefully defined performance priorities. There is a difference between an industrial show that is primarily a celebration and a show that utilizes theatricality to emotionalize critical business issues. See Figure 10-1.

Cost-effective impact can be achieved by modifications of circuses, ice shows, rodeos, Broadway musicals, Olympic competitive events, marching bands, and other existing vehicles of showmanship.

You want impact, speed, interactivity, retrievability, and economy in your media choices. It should be clear, then, that the best method depends upon your business applications. Every method has its advantages. While precise judgment revolves around considering specific methods for specific objectives, the chart shown in Figure 10-2 shows broad categorizations of high, medium, and low effectiveness for various media.

	Impact	Speed	Inter-action	Retriev-ability	Economy
Video Memo	M	H	L	M	H
Video Production	H	M	L	M	H
Big Screen Movie	H	L	L	L	L
Videodisc	H	L	H	H	L
Live Show	H	L	M	L	L
Computer Information	L	H	H	H	H
Classroom	H	M	H	L	M
Newspaper	M	H	M	H	H
Magazine	H	M	M	H	H
Book	H	L	M	H	M
Telephone Call	M	H	H	L	H
Satellite Telecast	H	H	H	L	M
Slides	M	H	M	H	H
Sound Filmstrip	M	H	M	H	H
Overheads	L	H	H	H	H
Charts	L	H	M	L	H
Audiocassettes	L	H	L	H	H
Props	M	M	L	M	H
Letter or Memo	L	H	M	H	H
Printed Report	L	M	L	H	H
Hologram	H	L	M	L	L
Electronic Mail	L	H	H	M	H
Fax Transmission	L	H	L	H	H
Compact Disc - Audio	H	M	L	H	L
Speech	M	H	H	L	H
Other					

Figure 10-2. Methods excel in various ways.

Communicating with Style

Style is an important characteristic of information streams. When part of the arsenal of a dedicated researcher and a logical organizer, style is invaluable. Without these other characteristics, style is a waste. When combined with content and audience insight, style is powerful to behold.

Words and visuals come in and out of fashion in the same way that apparel changes with the seasons and the times. Fashion moves as far as it can in one direction and then often reverses itself. For example, when skirts become long or short to an extreme, the hemlines may suddenly and radically move the other way. By the same token, the personality of communications shifts with the times.

You search for the new routine, the fresh phrase, the striking visual, to wake and refresh, to surprise, and to earn continued active, alert involvement. That's why talent rosters for business events include singers, dancers, double-talk artists, comedians, and magicians who can make problems disappear and literally turn red ink into black ink. All this is part of the packaging of professional communications. But it needs to be kept in perspective as only the wrapping. Inside the package, most of all, must be content and purpose. If the "act" is purely extraneous, then it's just gimmickry. When unique talent creates fresh insight, opens minds, makes a key point memorable, then you have used imagination purposefully.

An important part of style in business communications is to have a good ear for the language of your audience. Research such matters as reading levels. Communicate in ways that pick up the idioms and uniqueness of the language of the workplace.

The Power of a Properly Turned Phrase

It is part of our heritage to think about communication first in terms of words. Plutarch may have anticipated the stresses of our times when he said, "For an aching mind, words are physicians." And it was philosopher Ludwig Wittgenstein who said, "The limits of my language are the limits of my world." So words should be chosen with precision and care, for impact and memorability.

Every once in a while, someone manages to capture an idea so purely and succinctly that it lives in our minds for decades, sometimes centuries, even millenia. This is the objective in business—to capture the essence of the message with such economy and simplicity of language that people are moved to sustained action. Here are some examples of phrases that crystallized themes and to this day stick in people's minds:

- "Go ahead, make my day." Frustration and the thirst for revenge. Clint Eastwood in the law-and-order film *Dirty Harry*.

- "Read my lips, no new taxes." Fiscal policy. George Bush in his successful campaign for the Presidency.

- "The only thing we have to fear is fear itself." Hope, encouragement. Franklin Delano Roosevelt, facing economic depression.

- "I have a dream." Vision, justice, equality. Martin Luther King, Jr.

- "I have nothing to offer but blood, toil, tears, and sweat." Determination, courage. Winston Churchill.

The common characteristic of these phrases and others that have echoed so powerfully through the years is their ability, when used as wings for important ideas, to cut through the natural human defensiveness against information overload. They strike a chord.

Phrases calculated to strip away pretension and cut to the heart of an issue have been used with skill in live political debates, so that now, politicians as well as business people search them out.

Ronald Reagan's "There you go again..."

Walter Mondale's "Where's the beef?"

Lloyd Bentsen's "You're no Jack Kennedy."

All stunned opponents, garnered headlines, and framed the agenda.

When words are used to explain clear directions and powerful concepts, the impact can exhilarate and mobilize incredible human energies. But the foundations discussed throughout this book must be in place, or the words, no matter how finely polished, just add to the general chatter and are quickly forgotten.

Using Numbers for Impact

Number crunching plays an increasingly important role in business communication today. But in these days of widely available computerized information, what the world does not need is a raw data dump. Numbers can numb when they are poured out in undigested, undistilled, uncrystallized fashion. Too often numbers are used the way a drunk uses a lamppost, for support rather than illumination.

When you are using numbers to make or support a point, certain questions will help keep them pertinent:

- What do the numbers mean?
- What do they prove?

- What can I do about them to make them better?
- How can they be visualized so that key trends and comparisons emerge clearly?
- How can they be customized to an individual or a group to portray what is realistically controllable or changeable?

Among visual formats that can give numbers a clarifying impact, consider the following:

- Maps, color-coded, can portray a winning territory or function in one color, a losing one in another.
- Simulated dials can show computerized information like instruments in an engine room. At a glance, you can see that all key indicators are within target norms.
- Races—race cars, horses, or other icons—can show progress toward objectives.

For All Words' Virtues, Actions Still Speak Louder

Symbols and cues are part of contemporary communication. When a meeting is running past published schedule time, when visuals on the screen have shadows or other blemishes, when a room has been too casually prepared, when audiovisual equipment has not been prechecked, when presenters wander far afield—these cues carry a message of casual operation that will overpower any words about disciplined objectives you expect to accomplish.

Speakers at the lectern may employ high-sounding words to convey the importance of the people. But if, for example, the travel schedule to get to the meeting is onerous, or the accommodations are poor, or senior management is aloof during informal social interactions, those symbolic actions will convey a far more powerful countermessage than the one declared to be the cornerstone of the function.

Because managers today know how to speak, write, and compute, can do it quickly and fluidly, and have dissemination mechanisms of speed and cost effectiveness at their disposal, there is a tendency to say too much, too often.

Words, numbers, and symbols must be chosen carefully for impact, the kind of impact that leads to action and persuades and instructs so that people do things differently and better.

That is a very different kind of communication and learning strategy.

Choose an Environment and Create an Atmosphere That Reinforces Your Message

As Mama Cass sang:

Words of love, so soft and tender,
Won't win a girl's heart anymore.
If you love her, then you must send her
Somewhere where she's never been before.

Hotels and conference centers are the sites of choice today. They can provide an atmosphere of luxury and fun. That's fine when the presentation involves celebration and optimism. It may be inappropriate, however, if the intended message is a need for belt-tightening.

Give it some variety. Jaded palates don't apply just to food. Going to the same old place can often subliminally signal the same old message. The fact is, meetings can be held any number of unusual or exotic places:

Aboard ships	On airplanes
On trains	Outdoors
On the tops of mountains	In mine shafts or caves
At science centers	At planetariums and other museums
In homes	In retail outlets
At engineering centers	In manufacturing plants

There is no limit to the number of imaginative locations. Thematically tying together location and message, capturing the natural drama of your business by taking people behind the scenes to where they couldn't go otherwise, will stimulate receptivity to your message.

Conclusion: Taking It to the Jury

Eloquence, showmanship, and knowledge all come to naught if you don't focus on what's most important. Communicating for performance change can be compared to presenting a case to a jury. To clear the way for change—to persuade the jury—three things are essential:

1. You've got to understand the case.

2. You must know the jury.

3. You must put the key issues to the jury in a persuasive way.

Communicating for performance change is not bowling scores or routine press releases or sermonettes or slides or brochures. It's going in front of the jury, in front of people who have to do some things in new ways, and explaining what's important to them. If you're successful, they will become receptive to change and willing to experiment.

Performance change, when it comes, shows up in superior products or services and superior values. The media provide the routes to the mind, but the payoff in performance improvement is what people actually do.

Media can be a powerful partner to help you communicate and teach with impact, speed, interactivity, retrievability, and economy. Managers who get comfortable with the world of sight and sound that surrounds us will find themselves better able to manage, develop people, persuade, and lead.

We have only begun to see the potential. We turn next to how strategies for educating employees can be extended to educating customers as well, a trend that will accelerate as media evolve and merge with life.

Checklist for Change

☑ Present actionable information that will be acted on in ways directly related to success.

☑ Look at different media as alternate routes into the mind.

☑ Select media on the basis of impact, speed, interactivity, retrievability, and economy.

☑ Fit the medium to the message, audience size and need, and program environment.

☑ Use television as a window to view best practices, not simply as a stage to entertain.

☑ Aim for visual memorability, the image that changes the way people think about things forever after.

☑ Gain impact through a combination of business substance and visual power.

☑ For maximum speed, use live communication and streamline your program development processes.

☑ Allow individuals to interact, help formulate learning and communication agendas, and access what they need when they need it.

☑ Set specification levels to suit the purposes, from powerful epics to simple video memos.

☑ Use words, numbers, and symbols to help create understanding and ignite action.

☑ Connect words to concepts, fresh information and matters that are important to the audience.

☑ Search for phrasing that is different and will pierce the walls of cynicism.

☑ Use numbers that crystallize what you want and say why. Visualize the numbers so that the key concepts become clear.

☑ Make sure symbols and cues reinforce your message.

Apply the Learning

Rate the media you use on the basis of impact, speed, interactivity, retrievability, and economy. Look around you at your work processes and find several scenes and images that would add power to your organization's visual materials.

Take one page of an important report. Edit it for increased communication power. Format it in imaginative ways. Put the action step—what you want the reader to do with the information—in a box at the top of the report. Experiment with ways that numbers can crystallize and support ideas. Check how the symbolism of type, graphics, and paper texture reinforce the tone and underscore key points.

11
Follow Through with a Customer-Education Process

Everybody experiences far more than he
understands. Yet it is experience, rather than
understanding, that influences behavior.[15]
MARSHALL McLUHAN

The Complete Sell

The same steps that you follow to mobilize your organization, the same media that you use to train and communicate internally, can be extended to educating customers.

In the age of the intelligent consumer, neither the hard sell nor the soft sell is quite right. Satisfying customers calls for the "complete sell," the presentation mode that anticipates, diagnoses, and matches their buying requirements.

The complete sell is strengthened by media usage that differs markedly from the mission of advertising. Broadcasting aims at broad audiences. Its purpose is to stimulate interest. Narrowcasting aims at specific consumers at targeted times and may thus be considered an extension of face-to-face selling.

As mass media have become more cluttered, fragmented, and expensive, sponsors have sliced television commercials to as little as 15 seconds.

139

These short clips are then clustered with dozens of other messages. No wonder so many consumers zap out the commercials, especially when they are not in the market at that moment for the particular products or services being offered. No wonder advertising has now declined to about a third of the marketing communication mix, down from two-thirds a few years ago.

As marketers reconsider their mix of efforts, they grow increasingly aware of an irony: All this massive firepower is being directed at people who are not yet in the market, which includes the waste of talking to a significant percentage who never will be. A strategy of generating interest is certainly important. But when the buyer finally enters the purchase-consideration phase, finally gets serious and begins dialogues, the communication power and intensity often diminish just when they should be increasing. The additional irony is that even in corporations known for marketing acumen, there is often no real strategy in place to help employees convey the full product-and-service story with maximum power when it counts the most.

Of all the partnerships for productivity, none is more important than the partnership between businesses and their customers. When you give your customers what they need to make intelligent decisions, you significantly increase your chances of getting a favorable response.

Point-of-decision communication and learning technology are far more sophisticated and powerful than current application would suggest. When these elements are integrated with how an organization's members are trained, you find yourself:

- Educating rather than "pitching" customers
- Diagnosing and thus understanding how and why buyers decide
- Proving your points of superiority
- Reinforcing key points by consistency between what sales people say and what audiovisual proof documents
- Establishing longer-term relationships by staying in better touch through the entire ownership cycle

To train an organization, you must understand its work processes and how it earns marketplace advantage. En route to developing organizational learning and communication, you assemble a powerful resource bank. This chapter explores how principles discussed in previous chapters can also strengthen selling and customer retention. Putting maximum power behind personalized, one-to-one selling doesn't happen automatically. Here is an example of discontinuity.

The research group of a sophisticated big-ticket marketer lays out with great clarity the 10 important advantages of their products in the eyes of the consumers. The report compares how they stand in each category versus each competitor. The research includes consumer reaction to various phrasings of their advantages. Very impressive.

Now, visit their stores—franchises owned by independent entrepreneurs. All around you are posters and other point-of-purchase support. It's colorful all right. But the promotional support is not tightly connected to the carefully researched advantages. The visuals are not connected to how sales people have been trained to present the products and thus do not serve as the kind of reinforcing cues that they could and should become.

Customers walk in and out of such stores, bravely identifying themselves as "in the market," perhaps able to hum the current advertising jingle that attracted their attention, but knowing little more.

This is potentially the time of highest payoff; for the organization to come across with maximum power and coherence; for learning, technology, and product proof to come together; for the total environment to be a partner in getting a favorable response.

A remarkably high percentage of visitors to such stores leave unmoved and unsold. This leakage will continue until a customer-education strategy is put in place.

Developing such a strategy requires considering:

1. How customers come to market, the stages they pass through on the way to make their decisions
2. What buyers need and sellers need at each stage
3. How educational media and information technology can be of help at each step

Figure 11-1 shows the stages in the customer decision-making process, what both the buyer and the seller are trying to accomplish at each stage, and how educational media and information technology can be of important assistance in helping move the customer to the next stage.

Reach Out and Intercept

When customers first start to think about making a purchase, and therefore about the kinds of products and services you offer, you want to be there first. Among the most recent developments in audiovisual technology that make this possible are interactive video kiosks, computer databases, and portable demonstration devices.

—Interactive video kiosks in shopping malls, airports, and other

Stages of Customers Coming to Buy	Needs		Educational Media and Information Technology
	Buyer	Seller	
Start to think about purchase	"Is this a good idea?"	"How do we find and intercept?"	Outreach through interactive video kiosks, computer databases, and portable demonstrations.
Seek information, compare	"Do I know enough?"	"How can we give appropriate counsel?" "How can we prove superiority?"	Open houses using total environment. Expert systems. Audiovisual product proof, expanded inventory, experience of others.
Decide	"Am I getting maximum value?"	"How do we create excitement and commitment?"	Audiovisual sample of the ownership experience.
Experience ownership	"I want to be listened to and satisfied."	"We want to reinforce satisfaction and know immediately about dissatisfaction, respond promptly and make it easy to do business."	Audiovisual information centers. Customer assistance hot lines. Portfolios, instruments and tools that make the product or service more pleasurable.

Figure 11-1. How customers come to market and make decisions.

high-traffic locations thrust your organization out to where crowds gather routinely. They invite individuals to identify themselves as wanting to know more about a given product or service. Consumers use the keyboard to input their names, addresses, and product preferences. The touch-screen television answers questions, gives illustrations of product applications, and fans interest in a one-to-one setting, all with a degree of intelligence approaching that of a skilled salesperson. This should not be surprising, since the laser videodisc which drives the kiosk can be programmed using much of the same material used to teach sales people to present their products and answer questions. Moreover, the machine has more patience than most sales people. It will tell the full story every time.

Outreach kiosks can print specifications tailored to the individual visitor's requirements and are even capable of dispensing coupons that encourage prompt visits to the nearest store. As a commentary on our media age, research shows that claims delivered by this machine have higher credibility than the same claims made by live sales people!

—Computer databases can track buying patterns, predict when consumers will come to market, serve up names of freshly minted leads, including addresses, historic purchase preferences, and how current products and services are superior to previous purchases.

Warren McFarlan of Harvard Business School has studied how computer databases can add several points to market share when their outreach function is fully appreciated and utilized. McFarlan points out, for example, that almost half of the travel agents in the country are tied to American Airlines' Sabre reservation system and another 27 percent to the United Airlines Apollo reservation system. Creating the information screens, portraying the convenience or value of your flights on the first screens viewed by travel agents, yields enormous marketplace advantage. About half of airline reservations are made for the first appropriate flight listed. Ninety percent of the reservations are for flights listed on the first information screen, even though less expensive or more convenient flights may be buried in the subsequent screens.

To show the marketing advantages that can flow from customer-useful databases, American Airlines has the ability to strategically reprice its annual inventory of 4 billion airline seats—every day. More than half of American Airlines' total profits come from its Sabre reservation system.

According to McFarlan:

> Information technology architecture is redefining the roles of competition in airlines and many other industries, fundamentally altering the art of the possible, and putting the cost and performance of information technology at the top of corporate agendas.

So computer power for marketing support as well as everyday transactions is going to continue to grow in most corporations. Computerized information will provide the basis of extending "frequent flyer" consumer rewards into "frequent buyer" plans in supermarkets and many other retailers.

As this explosion of reusable, targeted information continues, data becomes an increasingly important resource to educate employees and to inform customers as they come to market. The educational concepts of "just-in-time learning" and "alternative routes into the mind" that we have been discussing should encourage you to begin shaping databases for learning to have follow-through application to consumers.

—Lightweight VCRs, lap-top computers, and other audiovisual units can bring demonstrations into prospect's offices or homes.

Provide Useful Information

As buyers start to get more serious, they want relevant information about a product or service. The kind of information desired goes far beyond the short, catchy themes designed to stimulate mass interest. Now prospects care about specific applications, features, and comparisons to their other choices—your competition.

—*Open houses* can use the total store or other business environment to present a powerful, coherent impression to carefully targeted guests. The movies, music, and other materials used in company meetings and classes can have valuable residual uses in events designed to educate customers to the benefits of your product or service.

—*Expert systems.* Computers have the ability to make sales representatives truly consultative. Inexperienced insurance representatives, for example, can respond with some of the insights and capabilities of the most sophisticated financial planners if they ask structured questions and if they are supported with computer databases containing comprehensive, personalized investment models. This is more than data retrieval. Computers, and video augmentation of computers, can teach ordinary people to give extraordinary counsel.

—*Product proof.* As customers get more serious about purchasing, they want to see how products can be used. Television and other audiovisual methods now take on their best applicability as media for dramatic demonstrations that take the products to the extremes of their capabilities. Photography, animation, or special effects can go under the surface of a product to show features, advantages, and processes that are difficult to describe with words alone. Interactive video allows the prospect to select demonstrations that precisely match his or her contemplated product uses. With simple props, salespeople can also conduct some see-for-yourself demonstrations on a desktop.

—*Comparisons.* Television, especially interactive video disc, and computer databases can provide pinpointed, head-to-head comparisons versus precisely the alternatives the customer is considering, addressing the purchase criteria that the customer is using.

—*Expanded selection.* Florsheim is an example of a retailer that increases available inventory through interactive video. When customers cannot find the shoe they want in stock, they can turn to a video center that shows the thousands of shoe styles in the complete Florsheim line, including current availability of sizes. Participating stores report sales increases averaging 33 percent.

—*Other people's experiences.* Of all the information customers gather, nothing is more important than hearing from other users. Point-of-decision audiovisual communication can let prospects select from a menu of applications and hear from other users who have faced similar requirements.

Make It Easier to Say Yes

No activity of a business is more important than increasing the base of satisfied customers, getting more people to be part of the family.

Even with the rich information assistance just described, experienced sales people know the challenge of moving the prospect from "just looking" to the signed commitment. The more expensive the decision, the more it takes something special to provide that final propulsion to say yes.

That something special can be to provide a vivid sample of the ownership experience, including capturing the emotional intangibles. Again, audiovisual technology has fantastic capability to simulate this experience today. While leading-edge entrepreneurs such as Carl Sewell, a Cadillac dealer profiled in *In Search of Excellence*, give customers audiovisual presentations, few if any companies have truly organized their selling processes around an all-out sensory experience. The tentative, ad hoc nature of most business applications of point-of-decision technology has kept the potential impact muffled. To appreciate the potentials, consider these trends in parallel areas:

- Theme entertainment parks are replacing some of the massive construction of blockbuster rides with audiovisual experiences that simulate these experiences in a smaller space.

- Science museums are bringing complex developments to life, luring couch potatoes away from their home television sets with giant "Omnimax" screens that curve over and around viewers. Theatres of all kinds will compete with home entertainment via spectacles of grand scale that immerse or surround the audience in the experience.

- Lines are blurring between real-life and circumstances recreated by media that are sometimes larger than life. At times, media is capable of creating the more memorable experience. The big-screen, technicolor portrayal of Paris with a 120-piece orchestra sound track may capture the romance of Paris better than the reality of a hot, crowded, noisy day fighting traffic in one of the less glamorous sections of this sprawling urban area.

Philosophers can certainly debate losses as well as gains to our life when media depictions of things and events become more real than the real. Daniel Boorstin, former director of the Library of Congress says,

> The tendency of technology is to make our lives...potentially more interesting. But at the same time,...it reduces the difference between everything and everything else, between every place and every other place.

Boorstin calls this a loss of nuance. So there will be some groping. But no force in our society is better equipped to apply media intelligently than business. And there is no more productive forum to pull out all of the experience-creation stops than with potential purchasers of products and services at the moment when they are most interested in those products and services.

It is remarkable that otherwise sophisticated marketers invest more and more money saying less and less to constituencies made up primarily of people who don't care, becoming more and more shrill in the process of trying to attract attention. Allocating some of those resources to telling the complete story in the most powerful way for those actually at the point of decision is an intelligent part of a contemporary marketing strategy.

Enrich the Ownership Experience

Some organizations are using an enhanced buying and ownership experience as a principal method of achieving differentiation. When a group, product, or service is new, there is a great opportunity to organize the business around customer-satisfying, customer-educating concepts. An example is the Infiniti Division of Nissan, which considers every phase of how it does business—from the teaching of its people to the architecture of its dealerships—as part of an up-level experience to which luxury car owners are entitled.

An organization can begin at any stage of its existence to rapidly incorporate such ownership-enriching methods as:

- *Audiovisual information centers.* These can update owners on imaginative applications from recipes, say, for a food processor, to self-repair tips for an automobile or other large appliance.

- *Customer-assistance telephone hot lines.* These can quickly flush out owner dissatisfaction and provide the fast response that prevents unhappiness from festering or spreading to others.

- *Education of the customer to take more responsibility.* This can save money. David Tansick, management professor at the University of Arizona, points out that in service organizations, the customers are involved in the production of a service. He uses as examples health-maintenance organizations that are training patients to perform some simple testing functions and tax preparers who teach clients to keep better records.[16]

- *Looking at work processes in partnership with the customer to streamline methods.* You get such a convenience dividend from hotels that allow you to avoid the checkout line by simply touching the screen of the television set in your room with responses that speed your exit.

- *Providing convenience tools related to product use.* Owner's manuals and other communications can be expanded from routine communications to impression devices and practical tools.

These methods, and others, boil down to making it easier to do business. So at each of the four stages of coming to market—starting to think about purchase, seeking information and comparing, deciding, and experiencing ownership—the learning principles and media methods that help train an organization can also be employed to educate the buyer.

Getting comfortable with educational methods and media techniques makes sense for the 1990s. When you add the dimension of looking ahead, seeing how rapidly even more advanced methods of communication and learning are emerging, you see the urgency of formulating a longer-term productivity strategy.

Conclusion: Anticipate Tomorrow

Among groups tracking the future of media are MIT and Kodak. The MIT Media Lab is making conceptual leaps in such areas as electronic publishing, speech, advanced television, movies of the future, visual language, holography, computers for entertainment, animation and computer graphics, schools of the future, human-machine interfaces, artificial intelligence, and data compression. Futurists at Kodak envision the following kinds of learning, organizational communication, and customer-linkage developments:

- The viewer asks a television scanning service to select highlights customized to his or her interest and store them on an erasable optical disc. A digitized text of news stories searches and saves the stories of interest to that particular viewer.

- Selected television images of particular interest are sent by electronic-image mail to colleagues and friends.

- The morning newspaper has imbedded bar codes to order merchandise directly from advertisers.

- Driving to a business meeting, the dashboard shows a detailed street map of the route from where you are now to where you are going.

- At the office, a handy six-pack of CD-ROMS carries 5 years' worth of product development documents.

- Researching a major new customer, retrieval includes video of speeches and news events.

- Erasable optical media will contain immense amounts of data and to a great extent will replace magnetic disks. Retrieval speed will improve dramatically. Low-cost digital storage of text, sound, pictures, and video and a variety of optical, magnetic, and some archival microform storage media will be seamlessly linked into networks. Costs per stored byte will be 0.000008 percent of what they were in 1960.

- Major metropolitan areas will be linked by massive-capacity fiber-optic lines, creating a vast trunkline for almost unlimited amounts of text, graphics, and video to be transmitted upon demand.

- Microcomputers on desks will have capacities approaching the mainframes of the eighties. Increased power will help enlarge, shrink, superimpose, dissect, color, and otherwise manipulate images. High-definition television graphic resolution will rival that of a glossy picture in *National Geographic*.

- The new technologies will be integrated into communicative networks—at the office, in the factory, at home, even at times in the car or the plane. Everything will talk to everything else in the data communications and electronics environment.[17]

Continuing cost reduction and integration of media will facilitate these and other imaginative uses. These are not predictions of some far distant future. The early phases of these trends are emerging clearly and being piloted now by innovators. Developments from this point on will depend less on technology and more on the imaginative uses to which the technologies are being applied.

The novelty of media will be looked back upon as our adolescence. Novelty will give way to sharply defined, carefully strategized uses. Media will more and more partner with human beings to accomplish specific goals. That approach to media does not have to wait for tomorrow.

Forging partnerships for productivity is life-enhancing and horizon-stretching work. It liberates. It stimulates with the zest of what could be.

That kind of excitement is important. Animating the organization with a sense of possibilities is part of the task of leadership.

We have moved from strategy issues to learning methods to media implementation. Next we turn to motivation as an essential element of productivity. Human beings will rarely accomplish more than they truly want to achieve.

Checklist for Change

☑ Extend education of the employee to education of the customer.

☑ Replace the hard sell or the soft sell with the complete sell.

☑ Analyze how your customers make their decisions and provide learning and information-technology support at each stage.

☑ When customers begin to think about purchase, reach out to intercept.

☑ When customers seek information and compare choices, give them help, information, proof, expanded selection, and experience of other users.

☑ Organize the selling environment to reinforce the reasons to buy.

☑ Use expert systems to give buyers sophisticated counsel.

☑ Trigger positive buying decisions with a sample of the ownership experience.

☑ Enrich the ownership experience with information centers, customer assistance hot lines, and other consumer education.

☑ Monitor emerging new media and information technologies.

Apply the Learning

Observe an occasion when your company and its products and services are being sold to the customer. If you are doing the selling, analyze your own portrayal. Make a list of the reasons to buy that are being used and an assessment of the power of the presentation. Now, make a second list. Put down all that you and those within the organization know about the product that *could* be important to the consumer. Inventory sights, tests, and experiences that go behind the scenes that could give dimension to those portrayals. Compare the two lists. If you sell, assemble the props, proof, data, and illustrations that can strengthen your portrayal.

12

Integrate Motivation with Work, Learning, and Communication

Most of the time we are only partially alive.
Most of our faculties go on sleeping because
they rely on habit which can function without
them. MARCEL PROUST

Partnerships of the Willing

Human beings use only a fraction of their abilities. We've all heard the stories in which a parent calls upon superhuman strength to free a child pinned under a heavy weight. We've all watched pro sports teams that seem to be playing full tempo turn up the intensity in the last 2 minutes to pull victory from the jaws of defeat. In business, it's not unusual for a selling organization to seem to be going all out, but then, cajoled by incentives or threatened by crisis, to dramatically increase results.

If emotion is power, motivation is tapping that power to achieve objectives. People put the most energy behind what they want to do. Formal motivational efforts, therefore, must be aimed at getting people to *want* to do what the organization *needs* them to do.

Partnerships for productivity are partnerships of the willing. They cannot be forged through logic alone. You want:

- Interior commitment that goes beyond mere lip service to goals.

- Something extra, from everybody, all the time—the something extra that you cannot get from surveillance or systems.

A Practical Definition

Motivation is the supplying of motives. It's giving the people you count on reasons to do what you are asking them to do. Those reasons must be important to the individual and appeal to the total person—to emotions as well as to logic. The reasons need to be connected to what is consequential to the business. There are limits to the number of things people get excited about. *Managing motivation is making sure people get and stay excited about what is important.*

Motivators and Demotivators

What energizes, activates, and motivates people in the workplace? Common sense will tell you that work itself, pay, status, benefits, promotion, perks, and recognition, among other things, serve as motivators. What demotivates people? The work, fear, failure, insecurity, the environment, and absence of incentives, among other things.

Pay and other forms of compensation clearly are motivators, but the experts tend to differ on the degree to which they are effective. Clearly, the absence of fair compensation is a demotivator, but good compensation seems to be taken for granted over time and, thus, becomes less stimulative.

Motivational Precept 1:
Motivate Prescriptively

Fish with Worms, Not Strawberries

Pioneer motivator Bill Power used to tell a classic fishing story, a reminder of the importance of getting the right motivators for the desired results. "I like strawberries," he explained, "and I hate worms. Strawberries with cream are wonderful. Worms just aren't. But when I go fishing, I put worms on the line, not strawberries, because the fish like worms."

Just as training should be carried out prescriptively, tailored to individual needs and wants, the objective in prescriptive motivation is also to be more pinpointed and personal.

Consider a menu of motivators—not just different rewards, but themes, counsel, and supports tied to the full range of attitudinal issues that your people face.

Continually Update Your Satisfiers

An essential point is that no single motivator should be used to the exclusion of others—different strokes for different folks. If the things that satisfy stayed constant, executives today would be walking around sucking on candy canes. Shifts take place over time for the entire work force. The following lists show how people who were polled ranked ten "satisfiers" back in 1946 and then again in 1986. The relative appeal of these satisfiers has been monitored at intervals over the last 40 years.[18] It is interesting to see how the ranking has changed.

Employee Satisfiers, 1946	*Employee Satisfiers, 1986*
1. Full appreciation of work done	1. Interesting work
2. Feeling of being in on things	2. Full appreciation of work done
3. Sympathetic help with personal problems	3. Feeling of being in on things
4. Job security	4. Job security
5. Good wages	5. Good wages
6. Interesting work	6. Promotion and growth in the organization
7. Promotion and growth in the organization	7. Good working conditions
8. Personal loyalty to employees	8. Personal loyalty to employees
9. Good working conditions	9. Tactful discipline
10. Tactful discipline	10. Sympathetic help with personal problems

Shifts in preference come not only as times change but also as individual employees move through various lifestyle stages.

Tie Motivation to What the Employee Makes Happen

A straight-talking businessman is interviewing a candidate for a key management position. The talk turns to compensation and incentives:

"I am cheap," he says, "very cheap. I sell 1000 units a year. I'll do that whether you're here or not. So I'll pay you as small a salary as I can to accomplish this company's current levels of revenue and profit, which I attribute to a valuable franchise, good location, excellent facilities, and years of hard work.

"But when you go beyond that first 1000 units, I become just the opposite. I become extremely generous because now we're talking about what *you* make happen. We're partners then, and I'll give you a share of the profits."

"What you make happen" is an important key to recognition strategy. What the individual accomplishes, what the team accomplishes, what support groups contribute—all need to be carefully evaluated. Recognition is a powerful elixir. Not only do you need fairness but also the perception of fairness by losers as well as winners. For recognition to be effective as stimulus for future effort, it must earn credibility.

Tap into Psychological Equity

Soldiers win medals. Football players proudly put decals on their helmets. Fighter pilots paint "kills" on their planes. Scouts earn merit badges.

Cash is not the only way to compensate. There are all kinds of perks, all kinds of ways to pay homage to accomplishment—cars, offices, trips. But they're wasted if conferred routinely for ordinary effort and if they overlook the psychological dimensions of recognition.

Just as entrepreneurs are motivated by financial equity in a business, every employee has a psychological equity in the position that he or she holds. That psychological investment needs to pay dividends just as reliably as would be expected from a financial investment.

Rosabeth Kanter, author of *When Giants Learn to Dance*, ticks off more than 75 novel ways to grant recognition and express appreciation. One imaginative suggestion, for instance, is to name intersections of your business corridors after high achievers.

Get Face to Face with the People Who Make You Look Good

When you want opinions, ideas, and reactions, who better to give them than proven winners? When managers sit down, if they do, with performers who have proven sustained mastery, the adrenaline can really flow. Getting successful workers to talk about what they did, how they did it, what they would require to do even better, and especially how their skill can be transferred to others to improve the total organization is a valuable company asset and a form of recognition in and of itself. When such master performers are taken behind the scenes, shown what is coming in the future, shown how their achievement contributes to overall company success, and then asked their opinions, the recognition is even more powerful and memorable.

Trends in Reward Systems

In a study of people, performance, and pay, the American Productivity Center/American Compensation Association and such corporate sponsors as Towers, Perrin, Forster & Crosby report that firms are searching for new reward systems that will tie pay to performance, productivity, and quality; reduce compensation cost; improve employee commitment and involvement; and increase teamwork and a sense of common fate. Of almost 1600 firms surveyed, three-fourths reported using at least one nontraditional reward mechanism.[19]

Nontraditional Rewards	*Total Percentage**
Profit-sharing	32
Lump-sum bonus	30
Individual incentives	28
Gain sharing	13
Small-group incentives	14
Two-tier compensation levels	11
Pay for knowledge	5
Earned time off	6

*Note: Column totals more than 100 percent because some companies use more than one method.

Employee involvement is another powerful element in a total recognition strategy. The same survey just mentioned shows half of the organizations queried using at least one of the following participation methods:

Employee Involvement Practice	*Total Percentage**
Team or group suggestions	21
Quality of work life programs	8
Crossfunctional employee task forces	20
Quality circles	22
Small problem-solving groups	23
Labor/management participation teams	10
Self-directed, self-managed, or autonomous work teams	8
Other employee involvement efforts	12

Note: Column totals more than 100 percent because some companies use more than one method.

Motivational Precept 2: Get Emotional about Challenge and the Change Process

When you are surrounded by problems, it is possible to overlook one of your most obvious motivational resources—the challenges themselves. In this day and age, people are smarter, more sophisticated, and busier. They respond more favorably to facts, figures, and evidence than to rhetoric, threats, and generalizations. In other words, proof can be an excellent motivator. The credibility gained by such an approach helps you maintain "share-of-mind" with otherwise inattentive audiences.

There is more significance to the staff reductions that many companies have been going through than just cost reduction. Jobs in most organizations are literally getting bigger. Realistically dramatizing the increased size of the responsibilities can be a powerful stimulus.

The key word is "dramatize." The issues that you face should transcend trend lines, pie charts, and data and should come alive as marketplace battles of vast importance.

Leverage the Emotional Part of Business Life

Too many managers in today's rational organizations tend to sublimate or deny the emotional side of life. "Don't get emotional" is a familiar rebuke.

Boake Sells is chairman of Revco Corporation and before that was president of Dayton Hudson. A forceful and articulate retailing leader, he epitomizes success, confidence, and authority. But in seminars on family relations, Sells pulls away the mask many people wear in business situations. He tells of a family life that was once in disarray, and the financial problems of Revco that preceded his joining that firm but resulted in the additional pressures of operating under bankruptcy law. The pressures forced Sells to the realization that all his life he had concentrated on the logical and analytical side of issues. He was impatient with people. During any of his onward-and-upward position changes, he and his wife would move briskly to tasks of relocation, with little pause to think or talk about how they really felt about what was happening.

Receiving counseling, Boake Sells to this day carries in his jacket pocket a list of feelings, under categories like "happy," "sad," "angry," "scared," and "confused." He is still learning to feel and to give this part of his life proper influence. So Sells refers to the list periodically to identify what he is feeling, very much the way a stranger to our universe might carry prompts about our language.

Communicate to Create Legends, Stories, Heroes

Business showmanship has its roots in the Roman legions and Camelot and the role through history of marching bands, drum-beat cadences, and bugle charges to bolster courage and ignite commitment. Communications today is more than a transfer of information. The aim is to emotionalize what is truly important, to reach for moments of fresh insight, to create new traditions and legends.

For example, an organization driving for leadership can set themes like "Fight One More Round," with the kind of get-yourself-up-off-the-floor attitude celebrated in the *Rocky I, II, III,* and *IV* pictures. The point is that ideas and values can be campaigned. In the words of Oliver Wendell Holmes, "Every idea is an incitement...eloquence can set fire to reason."

Motivational Precept 3: Tie Motivation and Learning Together

When people come together to learn, when organizations go on record regarding what they believe is important—those can be special moments worth seizing. If the motivational goal is to get "inside," so that people "want to" rather than "have to," you are looking for ways to enter the mind. It is during learning, meetings, and communication activities that the eyes, ears, and mouth are opened as pathways. Times of learning and communication are when individuals are in a receiving mode, when curiosity and open-minded consideration of alternatives are being stimulated.

Turn Application of Training into Competitive Sport

What's important about business learning is what happens afterward. Yet many corporations treat their workers and dealers to lavish perks for objectives that have little to do with what is being taught. Something is out of alignment—either the objectives or the curriculum. The two ought to work together. When they don't, employees come back from courses brimming with new product and people-handling skills that they use for a while, then drop because there is no reinforcement. If it's important enough to teach, and the payoff is in the application, then it makes sense to focus motivation on how learning is used.

—For example, good sales people are competitive. They depend on their ability to convey their product knowledge in ways that customers understand. Chevrolet and Buick are two organizations that have put these fundamentals together in an imaginative way with "National Walkaround Championships." Sales people compete at local, then regional, then national levels with selling presentations in front of live audiences to win important prizes.

—Domino's Pizza managers know a lot about competition; their chief executive also owns the Detroit Tigers baseball team. Domino's stages an annual Domino's Olympics. Employees compete for awards based on superiority in the exact functions for which they are paid, from making pizza dough to answering the telephone.

When you tie motivation to application, you stimulate a group of performers and you get an important by-product. By putting master performers in the spotlight—capturing what they do via video, audio, or print—you not only satisfy the egos of your best, you enrich your experience base, which can then be transmitted to others.

Reward Disproportionately for Breakthrough Action

Rewards don't have to be distributed evenly through time. Try paying big for the first time that something important is achieved. Tie training, application, and disproportionate reward for breakthroughs together. When you do this, you not only get incremental business results to fund the payout, but you get a long-term profit stream from the individual's realizing that the accomplishment is doable.

Every subsequent replication of the breakthrough achievement doesn't have to carry the big bucks and the big celebration—because it's a replication. The mastery is now part of that individual's repertory of successful behaviors. As George Bernard Shaw correctly observed, "A man's mind, stretched by a new idea, can never go back to its original dimension."

In effect, dare your people to do something great, teach them how to do it, and then be quick to recognize the achievement. You are making a bet that the individual and the organization will both win.

Stimulate Innovation

In a world of upheaval, investments in motivation should be applied to encourage people to try things not only beyond their previous experience, but beyond what *anybody* has done.

To encourage bold breakthroughs, structure "laboratories of change" to pilot new methods. Ask average performers to follow a set of principles and practices with superior discipline and effort. With cynics, ask for a willing suspension of disbelief, an honest following of the principles and methods you are teaching. Explain that in view of their concerns, they have been chosen to test premises and flush out problems.

While the spotlight is on this group, performance will improve dramatically. People respond to change and attention. And the methods you are advocating with laboratories of change will yield an important resource for motivating others.

The exploits of these freshly minted master performers, ordinary folks who became superior as others watched, have special motivational power if they are disseminated widely.

It's the same principle as some diet ads, which show not just beautifully slim people, but before-and-after photos of people who were stout and willed themselves into better shape. Laboratories of change not only capture and transmit superior performance, they give visibility to the stair steps you climb to move from average to exceptional performance. When ordinary people are given the means to attain extraordinary results, you sweep away a lot of excuses.

Motivational Precept 4:
Reward the Right People for
the Right Things at the
Right Time

Organizations that are sophisticated in other aspects of business make naive, awkward mistakes when it comes to recognizing achievement. Today, the people you count on are imbued with a sense of entitlement. Employees feel that when they have done things that merit recognition, they are entitled to timely reward, and when it is not forthcoming, that they have been short-changed.

The important step is to be precise and correlative in your recognition. Using good measurements, you not only need to know who you are recognizing, but why. And the recipients need to know as well. Just as important, the rest of the organization has to perceive the fairness, to understand that cause and effect are at work in your organization so that significantly increased contribution will reliably trigger a variety of reciprocal organizational responses.

The key is to match reward with accomplishment on a timely basis. This is important to the individual. The philosopher E. M. Cioran puts it this way, "If each of us were to confess his most secret desire, the one that inspires all his plans, all his actions, he would say, 'I want to be praised.'"

Sound, timely recognition strategy is as important to the organization as it is to individual recipients. No matter how decisive you are regarding your objectives, and no matter how much power you put behind them, you will not achieve sustained success without a strategy of recognition. The essence of partnerships for productivity is for every member of the partnership to get something out of the relationship, something that demonstrates that the organization understands and appreciates contributions.

The guiding principle is to promptly recognize incremental achievement, as achieved, on a precise and pinpointed basis, such recognition escalating in proportion to the significance of the accomplishment.

Overlooking Simple Cause and Effect

Some organizations put people in no-win situations where they have no control over what happens. That does nothing but breed frustration. The point is to recognize people only for what they themselves can do something about. A person who makes *car* parts, for example, cannot be expected to do much for *truck* sales, even if his or her bonus is hooked to sales.

There must be enough immediacy in recognition that recipients can see a direct causal relationship between the reward and the contribution they make. And motivators must be constructed carefully, allowing enough stretch to keep employees moving to the outermost edge of superior effort without going that inch further that leads to frustration because the prize is unattainable.

Remember What You Ask For

Sometimes teams are sent off to meet challenges with great flourish. The newest, most impressionable team members are amazed when their battle-scarred elders don't take this new challenge seriously. Those newcomers learn organizational reality when, after months of superior effort, none of the higher-ups seems to remember the assignment. They have become preoccupied with new initiatives.

Remember Who Won

With fanfare, Charlie or Sue win honor after honor, getting gold star after gold star next to their names. And then it's time for promotions, big raises, or bonuses. If Charlie or Sue are passed over while the financial gravy goes to others, it's only a matter of time before serious morale problems take hold.

Guard the Integrity of Your Recognition Currency

New honors and awards are created, given fancy titles and lots of glitz, but then aren't given time to establish long-term meaning through the consistent caliber of the recipients. The Congressional Medal of Honor is only a little medal and ribbon. Awards more physically impressive than the Nobel Prize, the Pulitzer Prize, or an Oscar can be purchased reasonably at your neighborhood trophy store. When new forms of recognition are first announced, the honor flows from the award to the recipient. But over time, that flow reverses. The caliber of the recipients, over time, defines the real significance of the honor.

Solo Superiority or Team Player?

There are times for solo recognition, when the individual ought to be accountable and shouldn't be allowed to hide in the crowd. There are other times, seen with increasing frequency, when only team effort will match the complexity of the challenge. It's important to be clear-eyed regarding when individual and when team contributions are paramount. Otherwise, you are vulnerable to sending mixed messages—meetings and training sessions that emphasize teamwork and appraisal systems that use forced rankings and thus ignore the intangibles of unselfish partnering.

Strategizing when you recognize the individual and when you recognize the team can open up your thinking to fresh pride-building, excitement-generating activities.

Conclusion: Make Motivation Part of a Total Process

Motivation that is mainstream to how an organization works, learns, and communicates, develops legitimacy, credibility, institutional memory, and sustainable satisfaction. Such motivation is a key element in creating the attitudes of continuous improvement. This attitude is captured by the words of a manager attending a mind-stretching academy on the campus of a midwestern university. Across the top of the feedback form, he scrawled: "Thanks for lifting the lid of that little world I live in."

In this entire Part 2, "Deliver Solutions that Help Individuals to Win," we have built on the strategic foundations of Part 1 and seen how you raise sights and expand worlds:

- Reach audiences of one with carefully targeted purposes.
- Set standards that clarify what you expect.
- Develop a curriculum that teaches how to meet those standards.
- Train prescriptively—tailor learning and communication to the individual by using the power of today's information technologies.
- Use media for learning as a way to see anywhere, to show best practices, and to educate customers as well as employees.
- Supply motives for people to take on the big jobs and bold breakthroughs.

Throughout the productivity-building process, you keep the focus of all the partners on results. We turn next to how to better understand what you are accomplishing, so that you can apply recognition and make systematic adjustments with reality-based confidence.

Checklist for Change

☑ Motivate by supplying motives—reasons for people to do what you ask.

☑ Motivate prescriptively, tailored to the individual.

☑ Continually update your satisfiers.

☑ Use a number of different currencies for reward—some as simple as listening and saying thank you.

☑ Get emotional about challenge and the change process.

☑ Communicate to create legends, stories, heroes.

☑ Tie motivation and learning together.

☑ Turn application of learning into competitive sport.

☑ Celebrate moments of fresh mastery. Reward disproportionately for breakthroughs.

☑ Stimulate innovation with laboratories of change.

☑ Reward the right people for the right things at the right time.

☑ Proportion recognition to the significance of the accomplishment.

☑ Remember what you ask for.

☑ Remember who wins.

☑ Balance individual and team recognition.

☑ Integrate motivation into a total development process.

Apply the Learning

Inventory the attitudes that stand in the way of the success you want to achieve, your organization's motivation activities, and the principles we have discussed. Develop a motivation plan—for your company, or your unit, or you may want to start with a plan tailored to your own goals.

Pinpoint one specific improvement for an individual or group. Find when the related knowledge and skills are next being taught. Offer an imaginative incentive for the immediate application of the learning in a way that produces an incremental result.

PART 3

Create a Self-Sustaining Partnership for Productivity

"Achieving results" is the objective of all the strengthening actions. But how do you know when you have been successful? Evaluation is not something that can wait until the completion of performance improvement activities. Determining accomplishment depends upon the original clarity and focus of what you set out to do.

Part 3 takes up the practical monitoring questions most frequently asked. Is the right team in place, and are the participants working well with each other? Are we spending money wisely, in a way to get a clear-cut return? Are we measuring and evaluating accurately enough to put a meaningful reward and consequence system in place and to make necessary systemic adjustments? Are there patterns to what we are learning? Where are the trends taking us? This inquiry will make you more confident and precise in evaluating how you are doing in developing others. You will see the pivotal role of monitoring so that new directions and necessary adjustments emerge in a coherent, energy-stimulating way. You will see even more clearly why productivity enhancement is not any one single activity, but a partnership of many forces and perspectives dedicated to self-sustaining improvement.

13

Blend Skills and Resources into Effective Teams

Competence grows under conditions in which it is required, invited, and nurtured.
SHOSHANA ZUBOFF

Empowering Teams

You will achieve results when your strategic objectives are clear and when, through training and streamlined communications channels and methods, the right skills are in place. The next important step to achieving significant change in performance is assembling teams and properly empowering them with sufficient resources. Why is it, then, that this step seems to take so long and involve so much confusion?

- Productivity improvement is a blurred responsibility in many organizations. It requires more than training or the effective dissemination of organizational messages. Line managers, staff specialists, business planners, and senior executives get involved intermittently. There are many ways to allocate responsibility for performance improvement.

Many companies have not made up their minds and fail to realize the consequences of indecision and blurred accountability.

- Contemporary performance improvement involves a wide range of skills and perspectives, and teamwork is a must. However, merging the personalities and coalescing the skills of a number of smart people into one harmonious, practical, useful thrust doesn't happen automatically.

- Drawing upon the various sources of outside expertise requires careful planning to get the most out of those capabilities.

Concentrate on Keeping Teams Fluid

Performance improvement is a continually dynamic process. Teams should be composed so that the balance of skills remains fluid. As projects move through phases and as longer-term requirements and objectives subtly shift over time, team makeup should shift accordingly.

Teams should have clear-cut charters and definitively delineated milestones of accomplishment. The men and women assembled to accomplish change and improvement should not consider themselves in rigid, permanent departments, but as members of continually rotating teams—sort of the business equivalent of a square dance. In the square dance, each member makes his or her contribution and then joins another "set" where those particular capabilities are needed at that precise moment.

Finding Your Place in the Accountability Triangle

There are many ways to organize, but however you assemble teams on paper, it is important to maintain the true spirit of partnership, in which:

- Skills are applied smoothly and imaginatively with a teamwide focus on results. Status and reporting relationships are sublimated to what is required to bring about a productive result.

- You assemble talents and perspectives to complement each other, making every effort to avoid duplication of accountability and territory. Stakeholders *together* represent the *required* range of skills.

Because focus on results is so important as the energizing force of partnerships, the task of setting clear directions is key.

In large organizations with ambitious productivity goals, there are really three levels at which direction is a factor—policy making, operations, and project. Each brings enriching perspectives. There must be involvement from every level. The responsibilities of each level must be clearly differentiated from the other levels. When all are in harmony, sharing objectives and values and interacting smoothly, this three-tiered review process is a powerful catalyst for change. When one of those perspectives is absent or inattentive, or when the three levels of review do not mesh, activities ricochet wastefully along a zigzag path.

Policy-level direction. Flowing from the highest councils of the organization, this is where human performance matters, if they're going to be, are best integrated into strategic agendas. The responsible senior executive is one who sees the corporate terrain in its entirety; understands the potentials, demands, and challenges of large-scale organizational change; and moves to seize those potentials. The policy-level champion need not be concerned about the details of project development or be a specialist in anything. The concentration on this level is to make sure that performance improvement efforts are tightly connected to key business strategies, to stimulate action, and to incubate innovation. The top executive makes it clear that the company will achieve competitive advantage through people, and conveys through consistent behavior that this is a priority, not just a platitude.

Operational direction. This usually comes from a senior manager who can direct a broad array of activities and understand how they fit together and when and how they should be sharpened, strengthened, aborted, or coalesced. On this level the manager's focus is on results and benefits, continually proportioning the effort and dovetailing it with all the other priorities that are unfolding simultaneously. The pragmatic operating manager is in favor of what works and wants training activities to pay for themselves plus yield a profit, with the payback occurring as rapidly as possible. This is the champion who wants to sell more of his or her company's products and services, cut costs, streamline processes, create new advantages—and who sees business education as the means to these ends.

Project-level direction. The third source of direction is the individual who lives with a given activity, sweats the details, fills in the missing links, sharpens the focus, and delivers on time, within budget, with clear-cut results. The project manager concentrates on the essential idea, the line of attack, and the assembling of resources—human and otherwise—inside and outside the organization. Project leadership breaks the project down into achievable elements, sets milestone reviews, and monitors accomplishments against qualitative, creative benchmarks with stringent control of time and money.

These are not necessarily full-time tasks. A chief executive officer may well be the policy-level champion. The head of sales, marketing, or manufacturing may be the operating directional leader. Outside specialists can assume some of these functions if chartered for turnkey results.

Consider the Full Range of Possibilities

Forging a business force is a dynamic process. You do not want a bureaucracy. When assembling teams, do a functional analysis first—even before you put down the names of people—and ask yourself: How much of which skills are needed for how long?

The importance of harmony and clarity at the top becomes increasingly clear when you consider the diversity of skills required for contemporary performance improvement task groups. Among the vast array of specialists that teams draw upon are:

- Operational realists, who understand customers, products, and services and the practical job pressures on the work force

- Functional specialists in management development, sales training, quality, product training, statistical process control, or other subjects being addressed

- Consultants, researchers, and planners who can conceptualize and recommend practical solutions

- Psychologists and other authorities on behavior, training and development, and motivation

- Instructional designers with the professional skills to design corporate curriculum

- Writers and other communications experts who can make points clearly in the least amount of time

- Information systems specialists who can create links between electronic hardware and what is being taught so that they reinforce each other

- Media specialists who can deliver learning in a wide variety of formats. Includes subspecialties such as videodisc, computer-based instruction, and other interactive visual techniques

- Instructors and coaches both in the classroom and at the work site
- Creative promotional talents who design work tools and supporting materials to bring the learning into the job environment—who keep the spotlight on utilization and application of what is being taught
- Administrators who budget, control, schedule, and coordinate people, time, and money versus milestones
- Specialists in evaluation and measurement who can document what is happening, what it means, and what to do about it
- Support people of infinite variety, from those who do the typing and schedule meetings, seminars, and other training events to those who ship and archive materials and can remember 7 years later where to find a replacement program element

Flush Out the Chief Alchemist

In Part 1, we discussed the importance of empowered leadership. Using the square dance analogy, the "caller" has the key role: to keep participants moving with grace and zest without colliding in confusion.

Another way to think about the program-integrator role is as chief alchemist. In ancient days, some people developed the reputation of being able to turn less valuable metals into pure gold. Truly significant performance improvement needs this kind of alchemy. Creative people with a range of backgrounds can be figured to have a lot of opinions. Somebody needs to synthesize them and keep things moving. Teams need to discuss, but discussion and data gathering can go on too long. Turning the corner from situational assessment to the disciplined creation of lean and practical solutions that achieve results is the intuitive, creative, value-added, integrative role that must be in place.

The alchemist may be the project leader, but that is not always or necessarily the case. It might be your creative head or some member of the team. The alchemy might come from an outside creative organization. This alchemy is what makes large-scale performance improvement part art and part intuition. The best solution for an organization at a particular point in time involves judgment. The program integrator has to know when to prod and when to pat on the back.

Where to Find Talent

When you put together teams to develop business solutions of any kind, there are four major sources from which capabilities can be drawn:

- Your own organization
- Specialty boutiques
- Existing, off-the-shelf materials
- Full-service training-communication agencies

What to Expect from Your Own Organization

What must come from within your own company are knowledge of your business, strategic direction, and the management of performance versus objectives. These cannot be successfully delegated.

All other task skills can be assembled from either inside your organization or outside or some combination of both. Inside staff is appropriate when there is a level flow of continuous work of a certain kind, when such skills are already on the payroll, or when the capability required is so specialized that the ready availability outside is not assured. Certain instructional positions can also be used as part of the career path of broad-gauged executives. Training others is a good way to grow. Helping people do a better job can strengthen leadership skills and attitudes.

When building corporate staffs beyond a nucleus, a question that needs to be asked is, What business are you in? Think through how communications, learning, and media specialists will be tied to the mainstream career paths of your organization. Specialized talent does not keep current automatically. Talent needs to be continually refreshed and challenged by a variety of experiences.

Getting the Most from Outside Expertise

As corporations become leaner, the line is blurring between inside and outside sourcing. However expertise is assembled, following are a few tips for getting the most from the interchange.

Tip 1: Get the Experts in Early. Companies waste incredible amounts of time and money fooling around with the symptoms of problems that may or may not exist. Capable outsiders can help define the situation and make recommendations. Their judgment may or may not coincide with your original diagnosis, but it is valuable as a cross-check in any case.

Tip 2: Listen, Invite Candid Counsel. Listen to what the experts have to say without cuing, blocking, or editing. You're paying, after all, for what they think and know. Remember, it is the client who is in control. The eventual decision about what to do, what to accept, and what to reject is the client's. But it's valuable first to listen.

Tip 3: Make It a Partnership. When groups or organizations work together in consortium, the seams don't show. When focus and trust are in place, people from a variety of units can work together smoothly to accomplish results.

As a sophisticated marketer, Colgate Corporation has evolved a set of principles for dealing with creative agencies. They were developed at the very top of the organization by its chairman and chief executive, Reuben Mark. These same principles apply as well to getting the most out of training, communication, information, and motivational organizations.

Colgate's ten commandments for working with creative organizations

1. Be the best client they have.
2. Really care.
3. Seek true partnerships and mutual trust.
4. Ask for excellence.
5. Give clear, honest direction.
6. Look for the big idea.
7. Streamline approval procedures.
8. Get the personal involvement of top management of both the client and the agency.
9. Ensure agency profitability.
10. Be human.

Many of these principles are good ways to manage anything. But when the mission is large-scale and long-term, requiring imagination and innovation, intermixing a variety of creative and operational perspectives, then it is particularly important to blend skills thoughtfully. Over and above the output that you achieve, the processes you follow to achieve sustained performance improvement ought to be a model of enlightened organizational practice.

What to Expect from Boutiques. A specialized boutique is a person or group of people who have become proficient in one particular area of business education, communication, motivation, or information. Boutiques might range in size from one free-lancer working at home to a staff of 10 to 100 people who specialize in one area of expertise. Examples are an industrial show producer, a television production company, or the psychology department of a local university. Boutique staff members are usually quite capable in their area of specialty. They gain efficiency by doing variations of the same kind of solution over and over again. Their shortfall is that they are answers in search of questions. Ask a show producer, and the solution is a show. Ask a professor and the solution draws heavily from his or her discipline of study. These are natural reactions. The responsibility is yours to make sure that the right questions are being asked when teams are being assembled.

What to Expect from Off-the-Shelf Materials.   Expertise today is frequently available in prepackaged courseware and other materials. Such training modules are generally cost effective since their development expenses are shared by a number of users. By coming off the shelf, out of existing inventory, they are tangible and can be previewed. Thus you get a very good idea of what you are buying. You can also check the experiences of previous users. Off-the-shelf materials are produced in a variety of media and span a wide range of quality. Some are designed to high standards. Others represent slick packaging and hype with little substance.

The major shortfall of generic materials is that, designed for wide audiences, they are not industry-specific, job-specific, or success-specific for your company. It is a poor bargain to save thousands of dollars in program costs, but then consume hundreds of thousands of dollars of extra user time wading through extraneous material. Don't forget—the most expensive part of business education is the time of the learner. Some producers of generic materials are developing methods and instituting services for tailoring material more closely to individual corporate needs. These tailoring services can run the gamut from serious customization to superficial repackaging.

What to Expect from the Full-Service Agency.   As performance improvement becomes a central success factor, you see the emergence of large, multidisciplined training and communications agencies.

Full-service organizations carry some of the same structures, strategic orientations, and values of a large advertising agency. The advertising agency works as a long-term partner to build a franchise in the minds of consumers. The training and organizational communication agency concentrates on understanding and developing the capabilities of internal publics—employees, dealers, suppliers, union members, and other stakeholders.

Just as a sophisticated advertising agency starts with customer research and strategy formulation, not ads, so a training and communication organization can help develop, in partnership with the client, an integrated, long-term strategy for change and performance improvement. In such formulation, the training-communication agency brings outside perspectives, cross-industry experiences, and the ability to ask the right questions at the right time. Usually, account directors have process tools for helping managers see beyond symptoms to root causes of productivity problems. By having a wide range of services, full-service firms can continually adjust their responses and deal from a client-in rather than an answer-out perspective.

Multidisciplined organizations can be good partners in reducing the overall number of communications events, helping make them flow together in a way that is more meaningful and that generates organizational momentum. The agency's repertoire of skills becomes more valuable over time as a long-run creative partner gains the insights that come from continuity. That same continuity can make sophisticated services less expensive than a potpourri of ad hoc solutions, because research and information gained on some assignments provide foundations for follow-on efforts. Response time is accelerated.

Full-service training and communication organizations will work with you in a variety of ways. Frequently, the relationship begins with needs-analysis research or one project. Sometimes that matures into a long-term, broad-based agency relationship; other times not. At times, the full-service organization is asked to assume an overall program-integration function in which some services are from that organization, but you may also choose to do some of the work yourself, or to continue the contributions of certain smaller organizations who have established themselves in a particular set of experiences.

Virtually all high-caliber creative organizations will work flexibly with clients and with other professional organizations whose work they respect. Most training-communication organizations will at times willingly use or modify some off-the-shelf materials, just as custom home builders today will utilize high-quality windows built in a factory. In such applications, the full-service agency generally has up-to-date awareness of the real strengths and suitabilities of existing materials and is in a good position to select or edit those portions of generic modules that are most appropriate.

Conclusion: Ask the Right Question

All four sources from which you assemble talent will coexist, just as they coexist in advertising, consulting, law, and other professional-service fields. As corporations seek outside expertise, managers often ask an incomplete question. They tend to ask, Who is best? The complete question should be, Who is best for us in view of what we want to accomplish? The key issue is the relevance of core strengths to your objectives. It is much more productive to probe these differences forthrightly, rather than ask for the stiff, superficial jargon of pitches, proposals, and "beauty contests."

The problems and issues faced by corporations today are frequently bigger and more complex than any one organization can address. Every creative organization needs to be willing to divide the work on the basis of "we do/you do/others do." Certain assignments, such as developing professional criteria, might best be served by industrywide collaborations. An example of this is the way insurance companies define, test, and certify chartered life underwriters on an industrywide basis.

Checklist for Change

☑ Consider the formation of the right team as a very important step. When the objectives are clear, skills are in place, and the team is empowered, you will achieve the results you want.

☑ Change the skill composition of your teams as projects move through phases and as requirements shift over time.

☑ Organize around three levels of directional perspective—policy, operational, and project. All three perspectives are important and enriching at key review points.

☑ Form teams that represent the full range of learning, communication, management, and support skills.

☑ Value the program integrator, the chief alchemist who can turn the corner from assessment and assembling of skills to practical solutions.

☑ Draw expertise as needed from inside staffs, small boutiques, packaged materials, and full-service training-communication agencies.

☑ Ask the key question, Who is best in view of what we want to accomplish?

☑ Create an environment for superior work.

Apply the Learning

List your major initiatives, the skills required, the skills you have in your own company, the outside capabilities that have earned your confidence, the gaps and how they can be filled, and the action steps to assure the right talents at the right time to achieve the productivity results you have in mind.

14

Increase Value—
Accomplish More
with Higher,
Faster Payback

Knowledge is the only instrument of
production that is not subject to diminishing
returns.   JOHN MAURICE CLARK

A Contemporary Look at
Value: People Are Your
Promise and Your Prosperity

Putting together alliances for productive enterprise is not a zero-sum
game. If you have a dollar and I have a dollar and we trade, we each
have one dollar. But if you have an idea and I have an idea and we
make an exchange, we each have two ideas.

A strategy to improve performance should be wealth-creating. It
should provide a better return than accepting the status quo. Derek
Bok, president of Harvard University, takes a rather commonsense posture on the issue. "If you think education is expensive," he says, "try
ignorance."

179

Time Out for a Declaration of Interdependence

We live in a world in which people are very protective of their inalienable rights. This book emphasizes partnerships because the century ahead threatens, or promises, depending on how you choose to look at it, a complexity unprecedented in the history of civilization. Only by working together will we mount efforts of the scope and scale required for meaningful change. In a world demanding productivity improvement, and especially when resources are being allocated to this end, companies and individuals have two paramount, intertwined economic rights:

- Management has the *right* to focus on incrementally superior financial results.

- Employees have a *right* to know what managers expect and how management will partner with them to help them successfully do the job they are being paid to do.

A Simple Test to See If You Have Your Eye on the Ball

As a manager, do any of the following questions sound like things you've heard yourself saying when it comes to developing your human resources?

How much did we spend last year?

Can we bid the job to find the cheapest supplier?

How many activities are we doing?

Business today is under enough of a cost squeeze that questions about money will be challenging. That's the way it should be. Improved productivity is supposed to add to—not subtract from—the bottom line. So be tough. But, as discussed in Chapter 13, ask the right questions. Here is a set of more probing and meaningful counterquestions to the ones just listed. Where do you stand?

Are you really satisfied with repeating last year's performance? Are your superiors satisfied?

Are you discouraging your resources from telling you what it will really take to develop serious, long-term solutions to long-term problems?

Are pages of text, minutes of video, hours of courseware the most important criteria? Who's paying for the extra time trainees spend being trained?

How to Get the Most for Your Money

When you are clear-eyed and consistent in what you expect and why you expect it, it is natural to want to stretch your dollars to accomplish the most with the least expenditure. Good news. There are ways to increase value, to make your money work harder. The extra time taken to lay solid foundations for your efforts, resisting the temptations toward mindless action, novelty, and disconnected flurries will reward you handsomely. Here are 10 ways to increase value:

1. Achieve results of consequence.
2. Save learner time.
3. Deproliferate marginal activities.
4. Avoid zigzagging.
5. Define the specifications.
6. Combine activities.
7. Design for multiple uses.
8. Provide predictable work flow to encourage investments in efficiency.
9. Adjust based on continuing feedback.
10. Share success.

Value-Stretcher 1: Achieve Results of Consequence

The best way to pass muster on funding is to make very clear that you are teaching the "profit ability" concepts discussed in Chapter 1. Address the abilities that bear directly on customer satisfaction, market share, and other influences on profitability. Make this consistently clear not just to the financial approvers but to everybody in the learning process.

Omit or make rare and responsible use of the platitudes that tend to creep into human resource discussions. Perhaps it is the legalistic environment that terrifies personnel departments, or the human potential values that are taught early in the public schools of democratic societies, but business education decisions are plagued by a disparity between what people say and what they mean. Sure, the legal imperatives are real and are important parts of selection, development, and promotion policies. And we are all grateful to live in a society that permits the individual to become all he or she can be. But in setting broad development strategies, you should not lose sight of the central thrust. In dealing with people, you are kindest when you are clearest.

Do Your Own Profit Ability Analysis.   Most companies are going to reach the appropriate funding levels by increasing their own comfort levels that expenditures are *investments*, not costs.

For useful analysis of profit potential, develop calculations tailored to your own situation. Figure 14-1 shows a couple of examples that can be used as patterns.

Once you have developed return-on-investment calculations that you have confidence in, don't just leave them on the backs of envelopes. In large organizations, many others are making decisions without good data. In the case of independent dealer organizations, you want far-flung entrepreneurs to see for themselves the self-interest benefits of employee development. Campaign to get the calculations that you feel are relevant into the computerized business-analysis reports that large organizations turn out today and distribute regularly and widely.

Put your weight behind getting the entire organization budgeting for results. Not activities. Results. If you are in a business in which the performance of people is a key success factor, if people are not performing to potential, and if you have good analysis tools, disseminate the hard-edge, practical mathematical calculations that give you and your associates the comfort of a reasonable return.

Educate Those Who Control the Purse Strings.   The kind of strategic, precise, targeted training and organizational communication that we have been discussing ought to be funded by improved results. In *Educating America*, Jack Bowsher recounts his experiences directing the training activities of IBM, budgeted at close to a billion dollars a year. Bowsher remarks:[20]

> Most executives view education and training programs primarily as an expense. This view allows increases in education budgets only during years of revenue and profit growth and demands drastic cuts during business downturns.

Bowsher puts the spotlight on a number of sophisticated, fast-growth companies that *do* regard education as an investment. And he recommends, "If you really want to bring executive focus to education, the

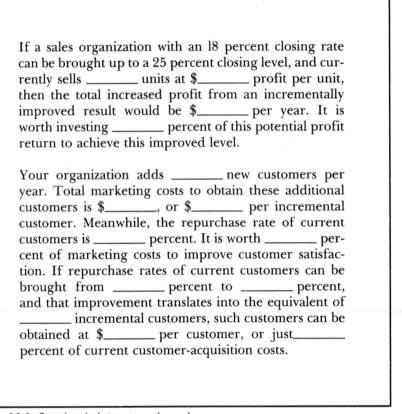

If a sales organization with an 18 percent closing rate can be brought up to a 25 percent closing level, and currently sells _____ units at $_____ profit per unit, then the total increased profit from an incrementally improved result would be $_____ per year. It is worth investing _____ percent of this potential profit return to achieve this improved level.

Your organization adds _____ new customers per year. Total marketing costs to obtain these additional customers is $_____, or $_____ per incremental customer. Meanwhile, the repurchase rate of current customers is _____ percent. It is worth _____ percent of marketing costs to improve customer satisfaction. If repurchase rates of current customers can be brought from _____ percent to _____ percent, and that improvement translates into the equivalent of _____ incremental customers, such customers can be obtained at $_____ per customer, or just_____ percent of current customer-acquisition costs.

Figure 14-1. Sample calculations to analyze value.

cost figures will make it happen faster than anything else you can tell them."

In this era of intense global competition and pressure to contain costs, it is quite natural for corporations to want to get the most value from business education. Of all the ways to analyze results, money is the method that will attract the most attention. You will not get the proper funding to hone your business force until you first educate those who control the purse strings. Value measurements are often quite different for education than they are for "things."

Astute financial executives can be good allies in justifying large-scale change if you can generate hard data such as current closing ratios, costs of absenteeism, scrappage, or other symptoms of waste, and develop credible projections of realistic incremental results. For example, quality guru and management authority Philip Crosby helps managers calculate the cost of nonconformance to specifications to show, correctly, that "quality is free."

Value-Stretcher 2: Save the Time of
the Learner

One of your most significant areas of economic analysis, and clearly one of the core principles of this book, is to save the time of the learner. Give the adult what he or she needs, precisely when needed, to be more successful on important matters, and make the learning immediately accessible to the individual, without travel and without waiting for a big group to form.

Value-Stretcher 3: Deproliferate
Marginal Activities

It should be clear that "results" are the thrust not just of this chapter, but of this book and the entire concept of partnering. Partnerships, consortiums, and alliances of the most unlikely bedfellows, including traditional adversaries, can be kept together when the focus is on results, on win-win incremental gains that benefit all of the participants. The commonality of interests, the interrelationship of profits, job creation, job satisfaction, security, predictability for suppliers, can be illustrated and campaigned when all of the stakeholders rally around winning.

Tough and consistent focus on results encourages you to deproliferate marginal activities. If you don't know where an activity fits or what it accomplishes, save 100 percent of the cost and effort. Mass your resources and your energies toward what is important, especially what will make a difference to your customers. Value what your marketplace will value because that's your surest way to get a reasonable return on investment.

Value-Stretcher 4: Avoid Zigzagging

Just as you want to save your own time and the time of the work force, so you want to save the time of your development teams and their outside suppliers. The biggest cost of program creation is the time of talented people. Material—paper, video, props, computer diskettes, and so on—are small parts of the total costs. Help your development teams move from point A to point B in the most direct way. The biggest waste in program development is wandering. It's like jumping in a taxi and saying, "Take me somewhere. As I look at the scenery, I'll decide on the destination." Meanwhile, the meter keeps ticking.

To avoid zigzagging:

- Decide where you want to go—what you want to accomplish.
- Make sure everybody understands not just the total task, but his or her part of it.
- Take the time up front. That's the least expensive, most important phase of program development.
- Schedule a few milestone review points and stick to them.
- Designate your deciders and tiebreakers. Deproliferate approval levels. Know what each brings to the decision process.
- Build a fence behind decisions. When you approve a phase, don't keep revisiting that decision at subsequent review points.

Streamlining developmental processes will not only save development time and money, but will increase your likelihood of a successful, profit-impacting outcome. When you reduce cycle time to implement any decision, you gain competitive advantage. This is especially so when you are dealing with human performance because the receptivity of the learner is so crucial. The closer the solution emerges to the situation analysis that triggered the development, the more it will be seen as responsive to learner needs and on target.

Value-Stretcher 5: Define Your Specifications

How much should a house cost? That depends on whether you want a mansion or a cottage, and on the kind of neighborhood you want. What we have discussed about A, B, and C levels of production (Chapter 10), and about dividing tasks and responsibilities into "you do/others do," applies here. Ninety-nine percent of all misunderstandings about costs are vagueness about specifications. To avoid such misunderstandings:

- Develop precise specifications in writing. Conceptual plans should be accompanied by tight, specific, unglamorous but important project operating plans—who will do what by when. If you are not certain what specification levels you want, ask to see examples of previous finished work to guide your choices.
- If you vary your specifications during program development, put dollars next to decisions. Ask for written estimates of cost implications before the money has been spent. If work is under way and proposed changes need your prompt reactions, make sure those reactions are forthcoming with necessary speed. Develop a quick response method to receive, approve, and record these changes in scope of work.

Value-Stretcher 6: Combine Activities

Many programs have overlapping objectives. Seek them out. Activities often can be combined, not only to save money but to improve focus and organizational power. Inventory existing activities. Modify appropriate off-the-shelf materials that can be used as building blocks.

Value-Stretcher 7: Design for Multiple Uses

Cascade materials down through all the levels of the organization, all the way to information that is usable directly with the customer. Teach the boss, then the subordinate, then the subordinate's subordinates from a common base of information tailored to the specific requirements of each function. Consider how other stakeholders who depend upon your organization could also benefit from your courseware, either as-is or with modifications. This not only saves money but is more effective learning. When various organization levels and partners share perspectives, they will team better, understand each other better, and reinforce desirable behaviors more effectively.

Value-Stretcher 8: Provide Predictable Work Flow

Wherever possible, drive down costs by encouraging level flows of work rather than extreme peaks and valleys. Predictability encourages investments in technology. It is natural for such investments to be more readily justified when the application of labor-saving devices is clear. This predictability makes sense not only for your internal staffs but for your key suppliers. Help them to help you. All suppliers who stay in business price their services on the combination of their costs and target profit. The really big portion of any estimate you receive is supplier assessment of costs. If you can help a key resource drive down costs, you can be the beneficiary through volume and predictability savings.

Value-Stretcher 9: Adjust Activities and Resource Allocations on the Basis of Continuing Feedback

Research, pilot-test, pretest, posttest—listen to your target audiences, not just at the completion point but all through the development processes. Listen to your developers. Let them air their concerns and questions. Allow them to suggest modifications that build upon what they are learning. Encourage an atmosphere of candor so that when something isn't working, people will tell you. That way, resources can be redirected to higher potential targets.

Value-Stretcher 10: Share Success

Reward users for applying what they learn to achieve incremental results. Incentivize developers for extraordinary work. Instead of bidding work, consider gain-sharing contractual arrangements so that all stakeholders benefit when better work can be done more efficiently. This is a form of contracting for results rather than activities. Consider consortiums of effort working against a master plan so that you develop some elements and, by sharing, earn the use of the work of others. Consider innovative residual uses of nonconfidential material, so that via royalties and user fees, you replenish your funding to do other good work.

Fuel to Fly

Many nations, industries, and companies underspend what is necessary to win. In a report entitled "Training America," the American Society for Training and Development (ASTD) reports that industry currently allocates 1.2 percent of payroll, heading toward 2 percent. This is sufficient to provide formal training to only 10 percent of employees. To give 30 percent of employees consistent formal training would require industry to move to ASTD's recommended ultimate target of 4 percent of payroll dedicated to training.

Conclusion: National Productivity Policies

Some of these value stretchers apply not just to organizations and individuals but to nations as well. A country that must increase productivity, that recognizes the role of education as the gateway to opportunity, that has been shocked by deficits and trade imbalances, should use tax policy, educational research, and reporting of economic indicators to stimulate productive action. Farmers are rewarded for growing crops. The most important crop of any nation is people. Some countries, such as Great Britain, collect and then manage the turnback of funds for prudently invested, industrywide training. At the very least, corporate financial statements ought to allow the capitalization of investments in people on the same basis as investments in brick, mortar, and equipment. Why can $100,000 for a machine go on the balance sheet for long-term depreciation, while $100,000 for people development must be treated as a current expense? These issues need imaginative thinking because business education is going to move more and more to the center of how nations become and remain competitive on a global basis.

Checklist for Change

☑ Concentrate on consequential actions, solutions that can deliver incremental results.

☑ Save big on the time of learners through dispersed, prescriptive learning.

☑ Eliminate marginal activities.

☑ Streamline developmental processes; move ahead in a straight line.

☑ Craft and communicate careful specifications.

☑ Combine and synthesize activities, to weed out overlap, focus attention, and add to strategic coherence.

☑ Design materials for multiple uses and layers of audiences.

☑ Provide predictability that encourages efficiency.

☑ Build in continuing feedback.

☑ Explore imaginative, success-sharing reimbursement mechanisms.

☑ Encourage industrywide and national policies that appropriately recognize people-development costs as investments.

Apply the Learning

Develop a financial case around a specific, people-dependent challenge or opportunity that faces your organization. Calculate costs and potential returns over time from defined, reasonably attainable performance improvements. Develop a recommendation and a budget in this format that emphasizes incremental results.

15
Measure Performance and Track Results

When you can measure what you are
speaking about, you know something about it.
LORD KELVIN

Not to Judge, but to Assist

Every step of performance improvement, from original strategy to funding, will be cloaked in vagueness if you do not have the will and the skill to analyze results. Measuring performance is at the very heart of establishing partnerships. Partners come together to achieve results and stay together when they see progress.

There is something in human nature that makes us care about what happens. Playing a sport loses intensity and focus if you don't keep score. Wandering in the woods is dangerous if you don't have a compass. By the same token, partners do not sublimate their individual cravings, look beyond their differences, or fold into the discipline of sustained team efforts unless there is some evidence that they are on a course toward a desired and desirable destination. All of the participants must understand:

- Where they are
- Where they are going
- How they are going to get there
- How they are progressing
- How it pays off

So tracking results is a very important step. It is not discussed until now because if you do not have the foundations in place, if you are not willing to sustain an organizational environment that will look candidly at current performance without searching for scapegoats, then measurement is premature.

Good Measurement

- *Begins at the Beginning.* While measurement is the back end of the performance improvement process, it begins far earlier. Front-end mapping of what you plan to achieve and back-end measurement and evaluation are parts of the same strategic process. Believable measurement depends upon agreeing about what you set out to accomplish.

- *Illuminates the Important.* When there is agreement on goals by all stakeholders, it is vital that the information flow illuminate what is truly important. With today's tools and information technologies, you have unprecedented capability to know about and share your understandings concerning human performance matters. Now that you can keep score with great precision and timeliness, make sure that what you measure is important. Measure what you mean. Recognize what happens—and who is responsible. The purpose of measuring human performance is to continue to improve that performance with an ongoing, systemic process.

- *Is Consistent, Fair, and on Target.* Keeping score consistently and fairly is a powerful mechanism to unleash the energies of the organization and to guide purposeful, continuing improvement. Keeping score casually and inconsistently will reduce levels of personal commitment and will curb the flow of innovations. Even more damaging than inconsistent scorekeeping are measurements that encourage actions opposite to those you intend. For example, if you want long-run thinking, be conscious of measurements that put their harsh glare only on short-run matters.

- *Converts to Action.* Data is not measurement. Numbers alone, which corporations can produce today in mind-numbing abundance, are not measurement. Data needs to be converted into insightful, actionable information.

- *Is a Path to What Can Be.* Keeping score is not simply the difference between what is and what was. It is an integral, dynamic part of the plan that lays out the path between what is and what can be. It is a practical tool that responds to the observation of Arthur Hays Sulzberger, "A manager's judgment cannot be better than the information on which it is based."

Measurement isn't for some abstract record. Timely, accurate portrayal of how you are doing is motivational for the work force. It is valuable for operating executives, to justify investments and to pinpoint future improvements. It is necessary for training and development professionals to continually improve content and methods. It is important to save time as well as money, to get the same or equal results faster and with more time for the worker to perform the job as well as learn it. Performance improvement isn't just "know-how." It is also "know-why."

Measurement by Anecdote vs. Measurement by Intent

Current practices of measuring and evaluating span a wide range. At one end is "measurement by anecdote"—isolated stories, casual samples, surveys of smiles and reactions. At the other extreme is a potpourri of complex, disconnected analytical techniques. Neither of these extremes is conducive to sustained productivity improvement.

Keeping score really involves a number of analytical processes going on simultaneously:

- *Assessment:* Do we know where we are? What we want? Why we want it? How we will achieve it? How and why it will pay off?
- *Prescription:* What should we do about what we have found?
- *Measurement:* What are the indicators we will monitor to judge how we are doing?
- *Evaluation:* What does it mean?

These terms describe subtly different approaches to what is happening. When an individual is trying to get a handle on a situation, these various terms and approaches can give dimension to thinking about the issues. But in large and even mid-size organizations, different departments, functions, and individuals may be using different terminologies, instruments, and reports. The result can be distortion, complexity, contradiction, and confusion. Individuals can be heroes and heroines on one report, laggards on another.

Integrate Your Indicators

If the major purpose of evaluating performance is to improve that performance, to give partners the guidance to make their own ongoing adjustments, then there should be an integration of the various evaluation tools and techniques. The list in Table 15-1 encompasses methods that are rarely looked at together. Some items are merely synonyms. The list is deliberately comprehensive to help you identify the various judgments that your company may now be making. Many organizations are unaware of the redundancies or gaps in their current measurements because the methods are administered by different organizational functions and hidden under different vocabularies. Inventorying a full array of methods is a step toward synthesizing a tracking process with increased coherence, consistency, and usefulness. So let's inventory the variety of analysis and tracking methods and then construct an example of an integrative model.

There are more methods, techniques, and questions than this inventory. In today's pressurized environment, managers don't need encouragement to be judgmental. The challenging part of tracking performance is to be responsibly judgmental, to give clear and consistent signals, to use data that is credible, and to make it useful to all of those who are serious about continuous improvement.

Develop a Model

As an example of an integrative model, Table 15-2 shows an approach that my associates have developed that we call Value-Test.

The integrative model, be it Value-Test or one of your own design, draws upon the full inventory of techniques and tools cited in Table 15-1. The Value-Test Interactive Model, Figure 15-2, begins to distill all these into fewer indicators that work together. This puts you in a better position to explain your tracking methods to employees and their managers, get their participation in the key calculations, load the information into easily updated databases, and help the participants at every level of the organization to quickly grasp key trends. Measurements be-

Table 15-1. Assessment, Prescription, Measurement, Evaluation, Action

Measurement tools, techniques, and/or commonly used phrases	Typical questions
Needs analysis	What is the problem or opportunity?
Situation analysis	What do people need?
Field research	What are people on the receiving end thinking and doing?
Literature search	What have others found?
Organizational competitiveness process	What are competitors doing better? Precisely? By function and task?
Front-end mapping	How can we visualize where we are, where we want to go?
Requirements process	What needs to be done?
Consultation	What experience-based, subjective interpretations would improve the understandings?
Customer satisfaction index	How do customers perceive what the organization is delivering?
Statistical process control	How can we use numerical analysis to see how we are maintaining process integrity, especially in manufacturing?
Financial reports and rankings	What is shaking out to the bottom line? Why?
Activities value analysis	What are we now doing that we should do more of, or less of, or differently?
"Profit ability"	What kind of return will we get on investments in organizational change? How can we translate involvement into dollars and cents?
Performance analysis	What do we want people to know, feel, and do?
Performance contracts	What agreements can we reach to achieve certain results?
Focus groups • Live • Telephonic	Qualitative feelings: What do people—learners, customers, others—want?
Surveys	Can you give us your answers to specific questions?
Job analysis/task analysis	What are the precise tasks of each job?
Gap analysis	Where are we now vs. where we would like to be?
Split sample	How is a control group doing vs. other groups?

Table 15-1. Assessment, Prescription, Measurement, Evaluation, Action (*Continued*)

Measurement tools, techniques, and/or commonly used phrases	Typical questions
Performance standards and evaluators	What is the standard for each task? What constitutes good, better, and best? How will we know when we have achieved it?
Systems approach	What is current performance? What is desired performance? What are the constraints? How will we measure?
Instructional design	What steps do professional courseware developers go through? Is it a training problem? An environmental problem? A support problem? What do people need to know, feel, and do to be successful?
Analysis of learner styles and needs • Psychological tests • Comprehension tests • Preference surveys • Adult learning criteria • Sketches, pictures	What do learners need to know? What do they currently understand? How do learners prefer to learn: hear, see, read, touch, feel, experiment, practice? How shall we teach? What should be group instruction? What should be individual and self-paced?
Performance appraisal	Is the employee job review connected to the important challenges facing the company? Is the employee being reviewed not just on the basis of "how good" but "how good on the things that matter?"
Delivery design • Reading levels • Media impact • User-friendliness • Interactive capabilities	What are the best methods and media for impact, extended use, cost effectiveness, time and travel savings, individualized learning?
Validation • Data analysis • Interviews	Does a test group understand the material? Are the tests correlative? Are they understandable? Do they measure what is important?
Pilot tests	How is the program working in its early development mode? What should be adjusted?
Environmental supports	What else should we look at? Supervisor support? Job aids? Technology support?
Reaction • Surveys • Samples • Interviews	How do users like the material? What do they want us to alter? Why?

Table 15-1. Assessment, Prescription, Measurement, Evaluation, Action (*Continued*)

Measurement tools, techniques, and/or commonly used phrases	Typical questions
Knowledge • Pretests • Posttests • Interviews	What do learners already know? How does knowledge compare to what has been taught and to what was known before the instruction?
Skills • Practice • Tests • Simulation • Observation	What do learners know how to do? Can they demonstrate mastery? During the learning experience? In their real-world environment?
Attitude • Tests and observations • Data collection • Interviews	What stands in the way of results? How have negative attitudes improved? Positive attitudes strengthened?
Application • Tests and observation • Data collection • Mystery shoppers	Are they doing what has been taught? • Immediately after? • At time intervals?
Consumer intention to buy • Interviews • Tests	Is the customer being favorably influenced by how people do their jobs, what is being said and/or shown about products and services, and the overall transactional experiences?
Results • Data synthesis • Split samples • Qualitative analysis • Consumer research • Remediation • Analysis of outcomes	What has been the impact on the business? Do customers see a difference? Is this difference important? What are the variables behind the learning experiences? What has been our return on investment? What will our return on investment be over time?
Recommendations for next steps Rolling performance plans	What should we do next? Where do new initiatives fit? What have we learned to give to future learners? How should we adjust the system? Who has contributed to success and how? How should we recognize and build on these strengths? How can we raise standards to create fresh competitive advantage?

come mainstream when they are quickly grasped and credible. Consider how baseball fans share the common vocabulary of batting averages, and how a fan who has not followed the team closely can be updated instantly through batting and pitching statistics and league standings.

Table 15-2. Illustration/Design of an Integrated Model to Show Flow and Relationships (*Courtesy of Sandy Corporation.*)

Performance objectives	Precisely, what are we setting out to improve and why?
Anticipated return on investment	If we are successful, what is the estimated dollar value of incremental improvement? Over what time frame?
Knowledge	What have people learned?
Skills	What can they now do?
Attitudes	What do they believe that is important to the tasks at hand?
Application	Are they using what they have learned?
Best use of learner time	Have we chosen distribution methods to save learner time and travel?
Business results	What bottom-line business indicators that the corporation regularly tracks are impacted by human performance improvements? What estimates can be made and ratios developed to portray relationships and trends?
Profit ability summary and next steps	A summary calculation, updated regularly, of the dollars and cents return of improved abilities and what should happen next.

Tie Results to Dollars and Cents

The language of business is money. If you can convert measurements to financial indicators, you will get the attention of senior management and move business learning from soft, intuitive, feel-good actions to the same kind of practical decision making that guides other organizational resource allocations.

This kind of economic analysis is very feasible today. Sure, there are many variable factors accounting for business results. But you can isolate those variables. And various kinds of training initiatives have different payback periods. But incremental results lend themselves to conversion into dollars-and-cents summaries. You can work with managers of various units to establish a ladder of performance improvements, and show the economic returns when individuals climb that ladder.

Make Measurements Diagnostic—Teach the Test

Some organizations and industries already have business measurements in place which have earned the spotlight. By way of example, the automobile industry has developed customer satisfaction indexes (CSI). CSI scores get a lot of attention and can influence judgments regarding candidates for valuable franchise locations. When certain indicators assume companywide or industrywide importance, it opens up a marvelous opportunity to "teach the test." Instead of developing a separate set of training indicators, build upon existing indexes and business measurements. Extend these measurements two additional steps. First, chart the specific people performances that alter the index (the speed and tone of the telephone operator, for example). Chart the range of performance levels from highest or most contributory to customer satisfaction to lowest, least contributory to satisfaction. Second, make the customer satisfaction index diagnostic by guiding employees and their managers to the learning, and the sources of that learning, that will improve performance and thus, over time, improve customer satisfaction.

You can frequently begin your measurement model with existing indexes and indicators because virtually all variable results in business are dependent upon how human beings perform. If your organization already has some sacred tests and hurdles in place, and everybody considers them important, then utilize that habit of paying attention. "Teach the test," design business education measurements that can be understood as a way to improve those operating indicators.

Be Fair in Holding People Accountable

Hold people accountable only for those measures within their control. Nothing is more devastating to an individual or to a team than to be ranked, scored, appraised, rated, or otherwise evaluated on random criteria.

In his quality seminars, W. Edwards Deming has a humorous routine with red beads, signifying quality deviations, and black beads, signifying acceptable performance, being scooped out of bins using a special-purpose tool. He has participants demonstrate this random-chance exercise and then lavishes exaggerated praise on those with more black beads. As the exercise is repeated, it becomes ironically clear that those praised and those rebuked have very little contribution to the distribution of red and black beads.

Make Measurements Graphically Clear

Whatever the measurement tools, key indicators should be shown graphically. Via simple dials or colored maps, stakeholders should quickly grasp where they are. Detail can be layered. But when measurements are used to stimulate action, it is important to present clear, vivid snapshots, especially for time-short senior executives.

This isn't just a case of crisp graphics. The challenging part of the process is to visually integrate the various indicators that tend to proliferate in companies today. To get the total organization moving in the same direction, get the measurement arrows going in the same direction.

Consider Technology Potentials in the Measurement Process

When you establish a consistent format, you are in a position to take advantage of today's information technologies to give you rapid, continuing updates to put data next to decisions.

Here are some examples of these rapid-feedback technologies:

- *Interactive Tutors.* Interactive videodisc and computers not only branch and teach on an individualized basis, but they can keep accurate records of program use, learning time, pretest and posttest achievement levels, and program difficulties and shortfalls. Such group records are useful for certification, including meeting such government standards as OSHA requirements.

- *Touchtone Telephone Testing.* Quizzes can be taken via long-distance 800 numbers. You respond to prerecorded questions by pressing different numbers on your telephone. Wrong answers can activate immediate prerecorded telephonic coaching.

- *Telephonic Focus Groups.* For cost-effective qualitative research, simply use conference-calling techniques. A preselected group of people can discuss a topic from the convenience of their home or office.

- *Computerized Gaming Simulations.* Specific business challenge games

can be designed to let learners make immediate application choices and
see results.

- *Role-Play Simulators.* Video cameras, computers, videocassette recorders, and television sets can be combined with simulation software
  to present specific challenges, video record instant learner response,
  and compare the response to highest capability responses.

- *Electronic Scoreboards.* In big-league sports parks, the electronic
  scoreboard is now part of the show. It is not just to record data but to
  portray heroes and simulate fireworks. Organizations that are clear
  on how they win and that involve all the stakeholders can give vivid,
  current portrayals of how the team is doing versus competitors and
  versus objectives.

- *Response Pads at Learner Fingertips.* These can capture immediate
  feedback, composite group reactions with colorful computerized
  graphics, and make presentations more interactive.

The technology of measurement is advancing rapidly. A. C. Nielsen
and the David Sarnoff Research Center are working on "passive people
meters." Their measurement services of television viewing habits will
soon be augmented by scanners that can tell who is entering the room,
and can store images of the facial features of viewers. So Nielsen track-
ers at distant locations will be able to discern not just whether the television monitor is on, but who is really paying attention.[21]

Instant, colorful visual technology will enhance the penchant of companies to "keep score" and the desire of serious, achievement-oriented
and competitive individuals to "move the needle." It becomes increasingly important, then, that the needle, the indicator that proclaims accomplishment, be truly connected to the job and to what management
really cares about.

Conclusion: Adjust the System

Consistent measurement gives you the information you need to make
pinpointed changes in objectives, tasks, people, processes, standards,
and supports. You do more of what works, less of what doesn't contribute.

Recognize Your Achievers; Help Others to Win in the Future

With good measurements, you are in a position to apply the motivational and reward principles covered in Chapter 12. You will be able to
demonstrate, clearly and credibly, that you have a timely and responsive

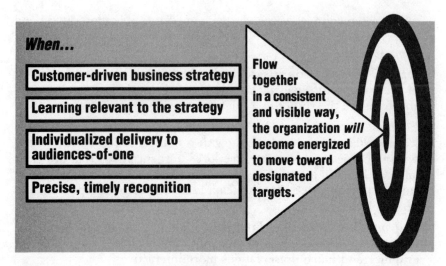

Figure 15-1. Develop a cause-and-effect flow.

reward and consequence system in place. You can demonstrate to your people that the principles of cause and effect are at work in your organization, as illustrated in Figure 15-1. Individuals can see their role in making good things happen.

Turn Measurement into Momentum

Keeping score provides powerful propulsion for organizational change. Over and above the joy you give people when you recognize their accomplishments, the locking together of strategy, learning, organizational communication, information, measurement, and motivation starts to generate momentum.

Momentum in many organizations is the precious missing element. Many companies and individuals who have figured out the right directions to move stay in the same place because there is little energy or intensity behind their intentions.

In the nineties and beyond, the emphasis must move from strategy to action. It won't be enough to have better ideas. The challenge increasingly will be to get those ideas into day-to-day actions with speed and consistency.

Of all the forces that can spark momentum and can continue to accelerate the pace of change, nothing is more powerful than recognizing the right people for the right reasons at the right time, based upon sound and credible measurements.

Checklist for Change

☑ Measure what is important.

☑ Connect front-end mapping and back-end measurement as part of the same process.

☑ Focus on the difference between "what is" and "what could be."

☑ Conduct a number of analytical processes simultaneously—assessment, analyzing the situation; prescription, determining what to do about it; measurement, how you track results; evaluation, understanding what the results mean.

☑ Integrate your measures; combine them with key operating indicators to give clear snapshots.

☑ Use the score diagnostically to help people understand what can be done to move the needle, in effect, to "teach the test."

☑ Measure individuals or groups only on what is within their control.

☑ Use graphics and technology to portray a simple, realistic, credible, continually updated snapshot.

☑ Use measurements to adjust objectives, tasks, people, processes, and standards.

☑ Use measurement-based recognition to generate momentum.

Apply the Learning

Take an important, new, people-centered organizational initiative and do front-end mapping of what you are setting out to accomplish. Develop the standards, measurements, and evaluators by which you will judge and share success. Develop a simple, graphic format by which your progress can be continually portrayed and shared. Wherever possible, put senior management reviews into dollars and cents, return-on-investment measures. As you undertake the activity, keep score, share the information, and initiate appropriate fresh actions using the measurements to support your recommendations. Reward key contributors for results.

16
Look Back to See Patterns

There are three classes. Those who see. Those who see when they are shown. Those who do not see.   Leonardo Da Vinci

The Pyramid and the Plow

Large-scale, sustained performance improvement requires an ability to see patterns. Today's workplace is turbulent and confusing. Those who aspire to take an organization from where it is to where it ought to go need to have an unobstructed view of direction, destination, and the root causes of past successes and shortfalls. When you look for patterns, you will find that they are there—the lessons of history, the experiences of others, and some immutable principles of the human condition. There are patterns of success. And there are patterns of repetitive failure.

Truly significant patterns are not always the most obvious, biggest, or most exciting. Civilization produced the pyramids, breathtaking to behold. The same period in human history produced the plow. It's clear in hindsight which development has offered the most contribution to productivity, the most good for the most people.

The Insights of History

It's wise to heed the insights of history because others have faced the anguish of change. Others have worried about what now worries you. Others have contemplated the thoughts, both positive and negative, that occur to those who lead people toward better ways.

"History is not the past, but the present made fresh."
Kate Grenville
"He who learns but does not think is lost. He who thinks but does not learn is in great danger." *Confucius*
"Those who cannot remember the past are condemned to repeat it." *George Santayana*
"That men do not learn very much from the lessons of history is the most important of all the lessons of history." *Aldous Huxley*
"The unexamined life is not worth living." *Socrates*
"The simplest and most necessary truths are always the last believed." *John Ruskin*
"The world fears a new experience more than it fears anything. Because a new experience displaces so many old experiences...the world doesn't fear a new idea, it can pigeonhole any idea. It can't pigeonhole a new experience."
D. H. Lawrence
"New opinions are always suspected, and usually opposed, without any other reason but they are not already common." *John Locke*
"Great men undertake great things because they are great; fools, because they think them easy." *Vauvenargues*
"Nothing will ever be attempted if all possible objections must first be overcome." *Samuel Johnson*
"Philosophy begins in wonder." *Plato*
"Man's mind cannot grasp the causes of events in their completeness, but the desire to find the causes is implanted in man's soul." *Leo Tolstoy*

> "Out of every fruition of success, no matter what, comes forth something to make a new effort necessary." *Walt Whitman*
>
> "In every age of well-marked transition there is the pattern of habitual dumb practice and emotion which is passing, and there is oncoming a new complex of habit." *Alfred North Whitehead*
>
> "Revolutions do not go backward." *Abraham Lincoln*

High Stakes and Life-Changing Potential

Since this book is organized to address the major productivity issues, the key premises are designed to heighten awareness of overarching patterns. So this chapter can serve as a useful summary. But the stakes of change are so large that something more than recap is called for.

Improving human performance is powerful capability with life-changing potential. How change is implemented and embedded can alter the affairs not just of individuals and companies, but of industries and nations. Our children and grandchildren will inherit the kind of economic landscape we turn over to them. The partnerships for productivity that we have been discussing are combinations of the free and willing, those who come together because it is in their self-interest. Preserving this kind of community is a matter that transcends commercial goals.

Coalescence vs. Compromise

The central issue today is *coalescence*—the merging of skills, the synthesizing of actions, and the partnering of capabilities so that the scale and power of the solutions attempted match the intensity and persistence of the problems.

Conversely, the causes of repetitive frustration—calling up images of the mythical Sisyphus doomed to roll the same rock up the same hill for eternity—occur in quiet, everyday compromises, underestimating what it will take to make the organization and its people consistently and visibly better.

At every stage, there are pressures and forces that stand in the way of purposeful, systemic solutions. Everybody wants the organization to win. Yet many intelligent managers who know how to bring out new products or cut costs can't quite find the levers of long-term, powerful organizational change.

Front-end coalescence, translating business strategies into performance strategies, is painstaking, unglamorous work. However, this is the highest payout phase, needing senior operating perspectives and the best talents in a variety of disciplines. Yet in organizations that prize action over thought, there is a restlessness to move quickly to events and tangible physical evidence of activities. Words and pictures are so easy to manufacture today that this rush to the glamorous part of producing "things" is hard to resist. But "things" unanchored to strategy, disconnected from careful analysis of what is truly important, simply add to the confusion.

Many corporations are not structured today to easily blend their strengths. Departments, functions, and task groups tend to have overlapping charters. When various streams of thought come together, frequently there is nobody playing the synthesizing role. Executives synthesize in areas where they feel comfortable. But human resources, as part of competitive strategy, is unchartered and uncharted territory in many companies. Many senior executives do not feel appropriately equipped, supported, or rewarded when they step into this breach.

Champions Face Demanding Tasks

Even when champions step forward, the process of clarifying expectations is demanding work. It requires precise thought and a widely scoped understanding of the total organization. Ironically, the leaders who could be the best catalysts are frequently preoccupied putting out the brushfires that repeat themselves because that front-end strategizing and synthesis have not taken place.

Inside the organization, the forces of change are not always understood and the institutional reinforcements frequently go counter to what anyone intends. The champion whose vision reaches beyond today and whose view of organizational requirements extends beyond turf and self-interest, who is willing to consider all that the organization must do in human resource mobilization to gain global competitive advantage, may immediately confront some colleagues who are not as far along in their thinking processes. Getting an organization mobilized to pack more of a wallop in the marketplace crosses turf, touches nerves, and asks challenging questions.

The Seduction of Instant Gratification

Just when coalescence becomes toughest, when the forging of authentic partnerships based upon trust seems most frustrating and elusive, managers hear the siren song of shortcuts. Novelty. Stuff ready to go. Immediate action. New initiatives. An exciting fad in human development—the business equivalent of the wonder diet. Slick packages. Slogans. Immense commotion can be unleashed at any time, giving restless executives a sense of progress. For those so tempted, the path is circular. After the sound and the fury, you are back where you began.

The pitfalls in serious performance change present themselves quietly, disguised as "good enough" and "easy remedy." Organizational or group efforts to improve don't crash loudly or in easily observable ways. When bold intentions are subtly gutted into tepid responses, the process is cloaked by politeness. Some people remain silent out of the sheer terror of recognizing how much has to be done. Some go along because business education that has been tamed to be less demanding is easier to take. Some who intend serious change simply are not sensitized to the nuances of these less familiar, and now increasingly important, human performance aspects of doing business.

It is to the potential champions of change that this book has been directed. It matters less where you are in the organization: what matters most is your appetite for real and lasting improvement.

A Quick Test of Improvement Awareness

The best way to summarize core principles, the quickest test of whether you have been alerted to what stands in the way of the kind of improvement you have in mind, is to move through the major steps of increasing productivity. See Figure 16-1, pp. 208–209. Note how each step is an important juncture, at which you leave yourself and the team vulnerable to the kinds of pitfalls that subtly weaken the effort, or you truly mobilize the major steps of increasing productivity. Pitfall or power… you have important choices to make at each key decision point.

Step   **Pitfall**

When you begin...   Activities get under way without focus, foundation, or context.

Human resource management is kept fuzzy and platitudinous.

**As you develop
solutions...**   Activities, events, courses, and communications spew out in piecemeal, overlapping, and at times, contradictory ways.

**As target groups
start to use the
assistance...**   Audiences are gathered in wasteful ways to talk to everybody about everything.

Employees, dealers, suppliers and other stakeholders bring their bodies to where they are invited, but withhold private commitments and the intensity that comes from such commitments. They simply do not see the relevance of what is being said or taught to the issues that they face.

**As resources are
allocated...**   Benchmarks of value are vague or inappropriate. In the absence of strategic context, bulk and novelty are valued, adding to the information glut.

**As change and
productivity
improvement start
to show up...**   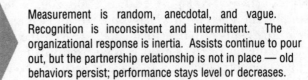 Measurement is random, anecdotal, and vague. Recognition is inconsistent and intermittent. The organizational response is inertia. Assists continue to pour out, but the partnership relationship is not in place — old behaviors persist; performance stays level or decreases.

Figure 16-1. Move through the major steps of increasing productivity.

You make clear that the objective is to create a "people advantage" — to use learning and communication to get people better at what matters to your marketplace. You build a base of customer-focused reality. You extend the business plan into a performance plan — what people need to know, do, and feel to achieve targeted results.

You put a priority on human performance as central to how you will achieve marketplace differentiation.

Activities are anchored to a larger framework, an ongoing systemic process of continuous improvement. The partners have a shared, holistic view of what is possible. Various functions and disciplines of the company blend their support behind what is important.

You create receptivity, earn internal commitments for action, and move the learning close to the learner, making help prescriptive and individualized.

Organizational communication and motivation are integral to learning — support what is being taught so those on the receiving end understand where they are going and why it matters.

You concentrate on what it will really take to achieve the level of improved performance that will show up in higher customer satisfaction, market share, profitability, and other practical return-on-investment indicators. Value is enhanced through streamlined process and saving the time of the learner by distilling the material to its essence.

You carefully track and measure what is happening vs. what you set out to accomplish; recognize individuals, teams, and units; enrich your content by monitoring leading-edge practices; continually adjust your performance improvement system based upon what you are learning, raising standards to increase competitive advantage. When you demonstrate over time that you are clear-eyed and careful in your human expectations, provide supports that are timely and relevant, and mean what you ask for, the habit of continuous improvement becomes embedded in the individuals you count on.

It's a SIMPLE Matter

Increasing productivity can be simple. What to do is known and proven. But doing it is not easy. It calls for consistency, credibility, and collaboration. Patterns emerge when you cut through the jargon and complexity and focus on what is truly important. Those who want to act on those patterns will find a willing and intelligent work force. Your people want to win. They need to be shown how. They need to be shown that you mean business—that their commitments will be matched by your commitments.

To crystallize the patterns in the barest, starkest, and thus most memorable way—to underscore what the three sections of *Forging the Productivity Partnership* really mean—let us close this chapter with the acronym SIMPLE. The three main themes of the book revolve around front-end, systemic, strategic foundations; making the learning interactive, individualized, and prescriptive; and measuring what happens. So you can recall the patterns this way:

S—Systemic

I—Interactive

M—Measurable

P—Performance

L—Learning for

E—Excellence

17

Look Ahead to Seize Potentials

Nothing else in the world, not all the armies,
is so powerful as an idea whose time has
come. VICTOR HUGO

The idea has come that the performance of people is central to all that we want to achieve.

Now, where do we go from here? Seeing trends early and acting on them quickly are the keys to gaining competitive advantage through human performance. Not only do you want productivity enhancement, you want the people advantage firmly implanted in the minds of your customers and other stakeholders in your business. You want the ways people do their jobs to be recognized by your marketplace as visible, important margins of difference. That means you want human performance practices to be in alignment with the future *before* that future becomes universally clear. So it is fitting to conclude by extending the trends to where they are likely to take us.

The principles discussed throughout *Forging the Productivity Partnership* represent the major thematic directions of the nineties and into the next century. Focus will sharpen. Developments will "excelerate" (accelerate toward excellence). But there is an important qualifier:

211

There will be some unanticipated problems as well as opportunities. Raising productivity is like climbing stairs, not like riding an escalator—it requires work. Nothing is automatic without the collective will to shape our tomorrows in the ways that are open to us.

The way ahead is emerging clearly. The decade of terrified introspection that business has been going through represents a massive sea-change and has yielded the broad outlines of the next waves of how we will live, learn, work, organize ourselves, and compete.

Our concentration on partnerships for productivity will be even more appropriate for the eras ahead. There is one central premise that makes partnering even more urgent and useful:

> Vast new human potentials are being unleashed by the swift removal of barriers, the opening of walls, both real and self-imposed. Geography, alliances, and relationships are being rearranged not just on maps, but more important, in our minds—in how we think about ourselves and others. We are moving toward a world of far fewer boundaries—a fact which will provide special rewards for those who think, plan, and act in ways unfettered by yesterday's limitations.

The Barriers Are Disappearing

Picture an urban aquarium that devotes part of its energies to research. Now picture a newborn yellow-headed jawfish in a large, specially equipped, experimental tank. The swimming space is divided in half by a tank-wide panel of glass. The fish strikes the glass repeatedly, learning the limits of its available territory for swimming. After many months, the glass is removed. But the fish now refuses to cross the line where the glass once was. Business faces this kind of dilemma, this kind of opportunity. The pane of glass has been removed.

With boundaries shifting or vanishing, yesterday's rules, maps, and charts are of little use. Explorers in the business realm must look again with fresh eyes at the real landscape. Vision and values—a clear idea of what is accomplishable—will be the cohering forces of partnerships.

Communities of people will combine to accomplish what otherwise would be impossible. Their composition will revolve around the knowledge, skills, and intangibles required for success. They will be formed out of a sense of common purpose, not because of legislation, organization charts, or habit.

Every major future trend that affects productivity pivots from this compelling, central reality that the boundaries are blurred or gone.

Seizing the New Potentials of Learning

As we head toward the next century:

- Strategy, learning, measurement, and recognition will build upon and flow into one another.

- Training, business education, organization development, coaching, expert systems, and other specialized pedagogical categorizations will be looked at under the broad umbrella of performance improvement.

- Learning in school and learning on the job will be part of a seamless, integrated, developmental experience. School will not be defined as a place, but as a process. Education will not be a time of life, but a lifetime concentration. "Just-in-time learning"—what is required by the individual, when required, in the learning formats desired, delivered instantly to where the learner is—will be available as needed.

- While government will retain responsibility for a broad range of services, more of those will be privatized. Some of that delegation to the private sector will be in education where instructional-systems design, measurement of results, and other attributes of advanced business education can help jump-start all that public education must accomplish.

- The mainstream concepts of employee education will also form the core of customer education, supplier education, independent dealer education, and union education. Sharing a common base of perspectives will provide efficiency and lubricate the human interchanges.

- What people know that is useful to other people will become the most important differentiator for individuals and companies.

Seizing the New Potentials of Work

Work, organizations to do the work, and the role of individuals withinthose organizations will all be significantly altered.

Organizational charts will be continually fluid. Reorganizations will be perpetual—ongoing adjustments to changing customer requirements and competitive challenges. Hierarchies and high walls between disciplines and functions will be seen as impediments and will be minimized. Adjustments of work teams and processes will be made closer to the customer and closer to the task by individuals empowered with information and encouraged to collaborate. The very fluidity of requirements will make partnering a fast, easy process because collaborations will not be seen as rigid or permanent, but expedient responses to the tasks at hand.

- Lines will blur between managers and subordinates who learn and take pride in the skills of self-management.

- Boundaries will be diffused between staffs and extended staffs. Corporations and their suppliers will divide tasks on the basis of skills required rather than conventional client/supplier relationships.

- Companies within industries will simultaneously compete and collaborate on issues that require the power and efficiency of industry-scale consortiums. Ambiguity of relationships—compete on Monday, collaborate on Tuesday, form imaginative strategic alliance on Wednesday—will be a more comfortable process because the partners will make joint decisions based upon marketplace needs and value-added skills rather than labels or traditions.

- Unions and managements will work together on growing the business, the surest method of job creation and job preservation. As part of ambiguity of relationships, adversarial self-interest positions will be asserted at contract milestones and over certain thorny issues, and then common gain-sharing perspectives will promptly resume.

- Country-of-origin of products and services will become increasingly hard to discern and irrelevant. This planet will evolve into a coherent global economic system with goods and services moving through various territories. Each participating nation or community of nations will add value in unique ways via high technology, access to resources, low labor costs, or other distinctive contributions. Regional and transnational governance mechanisms will grow in influence.

- There will be unity between realizing potential, expressing uniqueness, and doing well on the job. Work that challenges will be increasingly viewed as a means to, not a detour from, fulfillment. When economic, social, political, psychological, and theological streams of thought find more common ground, there will be a liberation of capability, soaring of spirit, and renaissance of innovation beyond anything we have known.

Seizing the New Potentials of Information Technology

Media and methods will combine and emerge in continually fresh forms as natural extensions of the individual.

- Real life and media will come together as a steady cascade of stimuli and experiences. Characteristics that we regard as the essence of humanness—humor, personality, infinite patience, concern for the individual, taking time to coach and share, and a sense of wonder, awe, and curiosity will increasingly be within the capability of communication and learning technologies.

- Information technologies like television, computer, radio, stereo, telephone, compact disc, and print will fade as primitive descriptors. New forms and imaginative combinations of solutional tools will emerge— continually lighter, faster, more versatile, and intelligently interactive, yet less expensive. Some miniaturized elements will be as small as today's jewelry. They will be worn as natural, personalized enhancements of human capability.

- Strikingly vivid images will make history and concepts clear and personal. Some visual and sensory happenings of colossal scope and scale will ignite minds, immerse individuals in simulated experiences that speed understanding. Humans will have the ability to view their work, their neighbors, their planet, their problems, and their choices from a rich array of perspectives. Because less will remain strange, there will be fewer strangers.

- Widespread access to expert systems will allow more people to replicate how the brightest minds think about challenges and perform tasks. Democracy will gain worldwide momentum based upon the ability to help individuals rapidly qualify to share opportunities and assume responsibilities. We can make real the social and intellectual mobility that free societies have yearned to achieve.

- Information flows will change and strengthen relationships, including ties directly to customers. Tomorrow's important highways will be from minds to other minds.

- The analysis and measurement tools that this book has emphasized and that sophisticated corporate leaders now use will also become the judgmental tools of the masses. Consumers will look back at the era of pitches, political rhetoric, and advertising jingles and wonder how their forebears could have been so haphazard in their decisions. Life will be rich in choices, and the role of education and communication will be to help formulate choices that are best for the individual.

Seizing the New Potentials of Speed Between Ideas and Applications

The most frustrating and wasteful boundaries to vanish will be many of the extraneous, time-consuming intervals between ideas and their implementation.

As needs are rapidly confirmed, process steps compressed and variables simulated, organizational responses will accelerate. This will happen not just through technology. People who know how to partner to achieve sharply defined results will gracefully form and break up solutional teams, secure and enthused that there are many more ideas to turn to when current potentials become reality. Fewer and fewer people will cling to "one way," as more and more people taste for themselves the richness and diversity of the fulfilled life. There will be a surge of creativity, contribution, and sustained joyfulness when more people get more confidence in themselves and their partners—when there is a shared sense of what human beings are truly capable of achieving when their potentials are unleashed.

The most important boundary that is being changed forever is the artificial cap on individual potential. The division between "haves" and "have-nots" on planet earth will ultimately disappear when all of us are recognized as having something unique to contribute and civilization learns, through partnering, to smoothly search out and utilize the best that is within all of us.

Source Notes

1. *The Guns of August* by Barbara Tuchman. Copyright 1962. Reprinted with permission of Macmillan Publishing Company.
2. Selwyn Feinstein, "Labor Letter." Reprinted by permission of *The Wall Street Journal*, (c) Dow Jones & Company, Inc. 1988. All rights reserved worldwide.
3. Wilton Woods (interview with Roger Smith), "The U.S. Must Do As GM Has Done," *Fortune*. Copyright 1988 Time Inc. All rights reserved.
4. Brett Fromson, "Where the Next Fortunes Will Be Made," *Fortune*, December 5, 1988. Copyright 1988 Time Inc. All rights reserved.
5. Sandy Corporation, *Customer Satisfaction and the Service Industry—A National Study*, (c) Sandy Corporation, 1988.
6. Jack E. Bowsher, *Educating America*, John Wiley & Sons, Inc., New York. Copyright (c) 1989. Reprinted by permission of John Wiley & Sons, Inc.
7. Richard S. Wurman, *Information Anxiety*, Doubleday Publishing Company, New York, 1989.
8. Randy Ross, "Technology Tackles the Training Dilemma," *High Technology Business*, September 1988.
9. Bernard Wysocki, Jr., "Technology." Reprinted by permission of *The Wall Street Journal*, (c) Dow Jones & Company, Inc. 1988. All rights reserved worldwide.
10. *Fumbling the Future* by Douglas Smith and Robert Alexander. Copyright (c) 1988 by Douglas Smith and Robert Alexander. By permission of William Morrow & Co., Inc.
11. Randy Ross, "Technology Tackles the Training Dilemma," *High Technology Business*, September 1988.
12. Michael W. Miller, "A New Picture for Computer Graphics: The Next Wave in PCs May Be the Use of Video," *The Wall Street Journal*, July 5, 1989, (c) Dow Jones & Company, Inc. 1988. All rights reserved worldwide.
13. Shoshana Zuboff, *In the Age of the Smart Machine*, Basic Books, Inc., New York, 1988.
14. Stewart Brand, *The Media Lab*, Viking Penguin, Inc., New York, 1987.
15. Marshall McLuhan, *Understanding Media: The Extensions of Man*, McGraw-Hill, New York. Copyright 1965, McGraw-Hill Publishing Company. Reprinted with permission.

16. Amanda Bennett, "Managing." Reprinted by permission of *The Wall Street Journal*, (c) Dow Jones & Company, Inc. 1989. All rights reserved worldwide.

17. Eastman Kodak, *Panorama, A New Vision of Technology*, Eastman Kodak Company, New York, 1988. Reprinted courtesy of Eastman Kodak Company.

18. Reprinted from *Business Horizons*, September-October 1987. Copyright 1987 by the Foundation for the School of Business at Indiana University. Used with permission.

19. American Productivity Center; American Compensation Association; Towers, Perrin, Forster & Crosby; and Xerox Foundation, "People, Performance, and Pay," Study.

20. Jack E. Bowsher, *Educating America*, John Wiley & Sons, Inc., New York. Copyright (c) 1989. Reprinted by permission of John Wiley & Sons, Inc.

21. Meg Cox, "Nielsen Announces New Technology for People Meters." Reprinted by permission of *The Wall Street Journal*, (c) Dow Jones & Company, Inc. 1989. All rights reserved worldwide.

Index

RANDALL LIBRARY-UNCW

3 0490 0390845 2